Computer Viruses Exposed: No More Infections

Beat Malware, Adware, And Spyware Now!

By Brian Mason

Computer Viruses Exposed: No More Infections
Beat Malware, Adware, And Spyware Now!

Table of Contents

Chapter 1: Understanding Computer Viruses.... 6

Chapter 2: The Different Types of Malware:
Virus, Adware, and Spyware 12

Chapter 3: How Malware Infects Your Computer
.... 17

Chapter 4: Recognizing Signs of Malware
Infection.. 23

Chapter 5: The Importance of Regular Software
Updates... 29

Chapter 6: Choosing and Using Antivirus
Software 35

Chapter 7: The Role of Firewalls in Malware
Protection 41

Chapter 8: Safe Browsing Practices to Avoid
Malware 48

Chapter 9: Avoiding Phishing Scams 54

Chapter 10: The Importance of Strong, Unique
Passwords 60

Chapter 11: Multi-Factor Authentication: An
Extra Layer of Security 66

Chapter 12: The Risks of Downloading Free Software 74

Chapter 13: Safely Downloading and Installing Software 81

Chapter 14: Handling Email Attachments Safely 88

Chapter 15: The Danger of Malicious Links in Emails and Messages..................................... 96

Chapter 16: Recognizing and Avoiding Malvertising 104

Chapter 17: Keeping Your Operating System Secure.. 110

Chapter 18: Using Secure Wi-Fi Networks 116

Chapter 19: The Importance of Regular Backups 123

Chapter 20: Securing Your Mobile Devices Against Malware 130

Chapter 21: Understanding Ransomware and Strategies for Protection 137

Chapter 22: The Role of VPNs in Protecting Your Privacy... 142

Chapter 23: Avoiding Fake Antivirus Scams 147

Chapter 24: Regularly Scanning Your Computer for Malware 153

Chapter 25: Securing Your Home Network.... 159

Chapter 26: Understanding and Using Browser Security Settings 165

Chapter 27: Risks of Using Public Wi-Fi and How to Mitigate Them 171

Chapter 28: Parental Controls and Protecting Kids Online 176

Chapter 29: Recognizing Social Engineering Attacks 182

Chapter 30: Ensuring Safe Online Shopping and Banking 188

Conclusion 193

Chapter 1: Understanding Computer Viruses

In the realm of cybersecurity, understanding computer viruses is crucial for anyone looking to protect their digital life. A computer virus is a type of malicious software, or malware, that attaches itself to a legitimate program or file and spreads from one computer to another, often without the user's knowledge. Unlike other forms of malware, viruses require human action to propagate, such as running an infected program or opening an infected file.

The term "virus" was first used in the 1980s, inspired by biological viruses that infect living organisms. Just as a biological virus needs a host cell to replicate, a computer virus needs a host program to function. Once a virus has successfully infiltrated a system, it can execute various malicious activities, ranging from displaying annoying messages to corrupting or stealing sensitive data.

Viruses are classified into several types, each with distinct characteristics and methods of infection. The most common types include file infectors, macro viruses, boot sector viruses, and polymorphic viruses. File infectors attach themselves to executable files (.exe) and spread when the infected program is run. Macro viruses, on the other hand, target applications that use macros, such as Microsoft Word or Excel. These viruses are embedded within documents and execute their malicious code when the document is opened. Boot sector viruses infect the master boot record of a computer's hard drive or removable storage device. They are particularly insidious because they execute before the operating system even loads, making them difficult to detect and remove. Polymorphic viruses are the most sophisticated type, as they can alter their code each time they infect a new file, evading detection by traditional antivirus software.

Understanding how viruses spread is essential for devising effective protection strategies. Viruses can spread through various vectors, including email attachments, malicious websites, removable media, and software downloads. Email remains one of the most common methods of virus transmission. Cybercriminals often use phishing techniques to trick users into opening infected attachments or clicking on malicious links. Once the attachment is opened, the virus can execute its payload and spread to other files or systems.

Malicious websites are another common vector for virus transmission. These websites may host drive-by downloads, which automatically download and execute malware when a user visits the site.

Cybercriminals can also compromise legitimate websites to serve malware, making it challenging for users to distinguish between safe and dangerous sites.

Removable media, such as USB drives, can also be carriers of viruses. When an infected device is plugged into a computer, the virus can transfer to the host system and begin its malicious activities. This method is particularly effective in environments where computers are frequently shared or where security measures are lax.

Software downloads, especially from unofficial or suspicious sources, pose a significant risk as well. Users may inadvertently download infected programs or files, giving the virus a foothold on their system. It is crucial to download software only from reputable sources and to verify the integrity of the files before installation.

The impact of a virus infection can range from minor annoyances to severe consequences. At the lower end of the spectrum, viruses may display annoying messages, cause system slowdowns, or corrupt files. However, more malicious viruses can steal sensitive information, such as passwords, credit card numbers, and personal data. They can also render systems unusable by corrupting critical files or disabling essential services.

The financial impact of a virus infection can be substantial. Businesses may suffer significant losses due to downtime, data breaches, and the cost of remediation. For individuals, a virus infection can lead to identity theft, financial loss, and a loss of privacy. The emotional toll of dealing with a virus infection should not be underestimated, as it can cause significant stress and anxiety.

Preventing virus infections requires a multi-layered approach. One of the most effective measures is to install and maintain reputable antivirus software. Antivirus programs work by scanning files and programs for known virus signatures and behaviors. When a virus is detected, the software can quarantine or remove the malicious file, preventing it from causing harm. Regular updates are crucial, as new viruses are constantly being developed and released into the wild.

In addition to antivirus software, a robust firewall can provide an additional layer of protection. Firewalls monitor incoming and outgoing network traffic, blocking suspicious activity that may indicate a virus infection. They can also prevent unauthorized access to a system, reducing the risk of a virus spreading across a network.

Keeping software and operating systems up to date is another critical aspect of virus prevention. Software developers frequently release patches and updates to address security vulnerabilities that viruses can exploit. By regularly updating software, users can close these security gaps and reduce the risk of infection.

Safe browsing habits are also essential. Users should avoid clicking on suspicious links, downloading files from untrusted sources, and visiting questionable websites. Email attachments from unknown senders should be treated with caution, and phishing attempts should be reported to relevant authorities.

Education and awareness are perhaps the most potent tools in the fight against computer viruses. By understanding how viruses work and how they spread, users can make informed decisions that reduce their risk of infection. Cybersecurity training for employees can also help organizations protect their networks and data from virus attacks.

In conclusion, understanding computer viruses is a fundamental aspect of cybersecurity. These malicious programs can cause significant harm, but with the right knowledge and preventive measures, their impact can be mitigated.

By staying informed about the latest threats and adopting best practices for digital security, individuals and organizations can protect themselves from the ever-present danger of computer viruses.

Chapter 2: The Different Types of Malware: Virus, Adware, and Spyware

In the vast and evolving landscape of cybersecurity threats, understanding the different types of malware is crucial. Malware, short for malicious software, encompasses various harmful programs designed to disrupt, damage, or gain unauthorized access to computer systems. Among the most common and impactful types of malware are viruses, adware, and spyware. Each of these has unique characteristics, methods of infection, and implications for users and organizations. This chapter delves into the specifics of these three types of malware, elucidating how they operate and how to protect against them.

A computer virus is perhaps the most well-known type of malware. Similar to a biological virus, a computer virus attaches itself to a legitimate program or file and requires human action to propagate. Once executed, a virus can replicate itself and spread to other programs or files on the same system or across a network. Viruses can execute a range of harmful activities, from displaying annoying messages to corrupting or stealing data. They are often spread through infected email attachments, compromised websites, or removable media such as USB drives.

Viruses are categorized based on their behavior and method of infection. File infectors attach themselves to executable files and are activated when the host program runs. Macro viruses target applications that use macros, such as Microsoft Word or Excel, embedding themselves within documents and executing their payload when the document is opened. Boot sector viruses infect the master boot record of a computer's hard drive or removable storage device, executing before the operating system loads and making them particularly difficult to detect and remove. Polymorphic viruses are more sophisticated, altering their code each time they infect a new file to evade detection by traditional antivirus software.

Adware, short for advertising-supported software, is a type of malware that automatically delivers advertisements to a user's device. While not always malicious, adware can significantly impact the user experience and privacy. It is often bundled with free software, enticing users to install it inadvertently. Once installed, adware can display pop-up ads, redirect browser searches, and collect data on user browsing habits to deliver targeted advertisements.

The primary goal of adware is to generate revenue for its creators through advertising. However, adware can also serve as a gateway for more malicious forms of malware, as the ads displayed may lead to compromised websites or prompt users to download additional malicious software. Furthermore, adware can degrade system performance, consume bandwidth, and create security vulnerabilities by exposing users to potential phishing attacks or malicious websites.

Spyware is a type of malware designed to covertly gather information about a user or organization without their knowledge. Unlike adware, which is primarily annoying, spyware is inherently malicious. It can record keystrokes, capture screenshots, access sensitive information such as login credentials and credit card numbers, and monitor browsing activity. The data collected by spyware is often transmitted to a remote server, where it can be used for identity theft, financial fraud, or corporate espionage.

Spyware can be installed through various vectors, including email attachments, malicious websites, software downloads, and even legitimate programs that have been compromised. Some spyware, known as keyloggers, specifically record every keystroke made by a user, capturing sensitive information such as passwords and personal messages. Other forms of spyware can activate a computer's microphone or camera to eavesdrop on conversations or monitor physical surroundings.

The impact of spyware on individuals and organizations can be severe. For individuals, spyware can lead to identity theft, financial loss, and a significant invasion of privacy. For organizations, spyware can result in the theft of sensitive corporate data, intellectual property, and trade secrets. The consequences of a spyware infection can be long-lasting, requiring extensive efforts to detect and remove the malware and mitigate the damage caused.

Protection against viruses, adware, and spyware requires a multi-faceted approach. Installing and maintaining reputable antivirus software is one of the most effective measures. Antivirus programs can detect and remove known malware, as well as provide real-time protection against new threats. Regular updates are crucial, as new malware variants are constantly emerging.

Firewalls provide an additional layer of security by monitoring incoming and outgoing network traffic and blocking suspicious activity. They can prevent unauthorized access to a system and reduce the risk of malware spreading across a network. Keeping software and operating systems up to date is also critical, as developers frequently release patches to address security vulnerabilities that malware can exploit.

Safe browsing habits are essential for preventing malware infections. Users should avoid clicking on suspicious links, downloading files from untrusted sources, and visiting questionable websites. Email attachments from unknown senders should be treated with caution, and phishing attempts should be reported to relevant authorities. Using ad blockers can help reduce the risk of encountering adware, while browser security settings can provide additional protection against malicious websites.

Education and awareness are perhaps the most potent tools in the fight against malware. By understanding how different types of malware operate and how they spread, users can make informed decisions that reduce their risk of infection. Cybersecurity training for employees can also help organizations protect their networks and data from malware attacks.

In conclusion, viruses, adware, and spyware represent significant threats in the digital age. Each type of malware has unique characteristics and methods of infection, but they all share the potential to cause substantial harm to individuals and organizations.

By adopting comprehensive security measures, staying informed about the latest threats, and practicing safe browsing habits, users can protect themselves from the diverse and evolving landscape of malware. Understanding the intricacies of these malicious programs is the first step toward safeguarding one's digital life.

Chapter 3: How Malware Infects Your Computer

In the interconnected world of today, understanding how malware infects computers is essential for protecting personal and organizational data. Malware, a portmanteau of "malicious software," includes viruses, worms, trojans, ransomware, adware, and spyware, all designed to infiltrate and damage or exploit computer systems without the user's consent. The mechanisms by which malware infiltrates a system are varied and often sophisticated, leveraging both technological vulnerabilities and human behaviors.

One of the most common vectors for malware infection is through email attachments. Cybercriminals use social engineering tactics, such as phishing, to trick users into opening malicious attachments. Phishing emails are crafted to appear legitimate, often mimicking the appearance of emails from trusted entities such as banks, colleagues, or popular services. These emails might contain urgent messages prompting users to open attachments or click on links. Once the attachment is opened, the malware is executed, embedding itself in the system and potentially spreading to other computers.

Another prevalent method of malware infection is through malicious websites. These websites are designed to look like legitimate sites but contain malicious code that exploits vulnerabilities in web browsers or plugins. Sometimes, even legitimate websites can be compromised to serve malware through techniques like drive-by downloads. In a drive-by download attack, simply visiting a compromised website can trigger an automatic download and installation of malware, often without the user's knowledge or interaction. This form of attack takes advantage of security flaws in web browsers, extensions, or outdated software.

Software downloads, especially from unverified or unofficial sources, also pose a significant risk for malware infection. Free software, pirated applications, and cracked versions of commercial software are often bundled with malware. Users seeking to bypass software licensing fees may unwittingly download infected programs, giving malware a foothold in their systems. Even legitimate software from reputable sources can sometimes be compromised if the source itself is hacked or if the software distribution channels are infiltrated.

Removable media, such as USB drives, CDs, and external hard drives, can also act as carriers for malware. This method is particularly effective in environments where multiple users share computers or when data is frequently transferred between systems. An infected USB drive plugged into a computer can execute malicious code and spread the infection. Some malware is designed to automatically replicate itself onto any removable media connected to an infected computer, ensuring that it spreads to new systems whenever the media is used.

In addition to these direct methods, malware can also spread through network vulnerabilities. Worms, a type of malware distinct from viruses, can propagate independently across networks, exploiting weaknesses in network security protocols or software vulnerabilities. Once a worm infiltrates a network, it can rapidly spread from one machine to another, often causing widespread disruption. Network-based attacks are particularly dangerous in corporate or organizational environments, where interconnected systems can facilitate the rapid spread of malware.

Social engineering tactics are another significant vector for malware infection. Cybercriminals manipulate human psychology to trick users into performing actions that facilitate malware installation. Tactics include pretexting, where an attacker creates a fabricated scenario to gain the victim's trust; baiting, where the attacker offers something enticing to the victim (like free music or movies) in exchange for their action; and scareware, which involves alarming messages or pop-ups claiming that the computer is infected and prompting the user to download malicious software disguised as a protective measure.

Malware can also spread through software vulnerabilities. Developers regularly release patches and updates to fix security flaws in software, but users who do not apply these updates remain vulnerable. Cybercriminals exploit these unpatched vulnerabilities to deliver malware. This method, known as exploiting zero-day vulnerabilities, takes advantage of flaws that are unknown to the software developers or users at the time of the attack. The effectiveness of these exploits underscores the importance of keeping all software, including operating systems and applications, up to date with the latest security patches.

Peer-to-peer (P2P) networks and file-sharing services are additional avenues for malware distribution. Users sharing files through these networks may inadvertently download infected files. Malware authors often disguise their malicious programs as popular files (such as movies, music, or software) to increase the likelihood of download and execution. Once downloaded and run, the malware can begin its malicious activities, including replicating itself to other files shared over the network.

Malvertising, or malicious advertising, is another sophisticated method of malware delivery. Cybercriminals inject malicious code into legitimate online advertisements. When these ads are displayed on websites, they can redirect users to malicious sites or directly initiate the download of malware. This technique is particularly insidious because it can affect high-traffic, reputable websites, making it difficult for users to avoid exposure. Users may not even need to click on the ad; simply loading the page containing the malicious ad can be enough to trigger an infection.

Lastly, legitimate software can sometimes be exploited to deliver malware through what is known as supply chain attacks. In these attacks, cybercriminals compromise the development or distribution process of legitimate software to insert malware into the software packages. When users download and install what they believe to be a trusted application, they inadvertently install the malware as well. These attacks are particularly dangerous because they exploit the trust relationship between users and software vendors.

In summary, malware infection occurs through various vectors, each leveraging different tactics to infiltrate computer systems. Email attachments, malicious websites, software downloads, removable media, network vulnerabilities, social engineering, software vulnerabilities, P2P networks, malvertising, and supply chain attacks are all common methods used by cybercriminals to spread malware.

Understanding these vectors and how they operate is crucial for implementing effective protective measures. By maintaining up-to-date software, practicing safe browsing habits, being cautious with email attachments and downloads, and using robust security tools, users can significantly reduce their risk of malware infection.

Recognizing the diverse methods of malware distribution is the first step in building a comprehensive defense strategy against these pervasive digital threats.

Chapter 4: Recognizing Signs of Malware Infection

In today's digital age, malware infections have become a pervasive threat, targeting both individuals and organizations. Recognizing the signs of a malware infection is crucial for minimizing damage and ensuring the security of your data. Malware, short for malicious software, includes various forms such as viruses, worms, trojans, ransomware, spyware, and adware. Each type of malware exhibits distinct behaviors, yet they often share common symptoms that can alert users to their presence. Understanding these signs can help in the early detection and removal of malware, thus safeguarding your digital environment.

One of the most noticeable signs of a malware infection is a significant decrease in system performance. If your computer suddenly becomes slow or unresponsive, it could be an indication that malware is running in the background, consuming system resources. This degradation in performance may manifest as slower boot times, delayed response to commands, or frequent freezing and crashing of applications. While there are various reasons for a sluggish computer, such as hardware issues or software conflicts, malware should be considered a primary suspect when performance issues arise unexpectedly.

Unexpected pop-up ads are another common indicator of a malware infection. Adware, a type of malware designed to deliver intrusive advertisements, often causes a barrage of pop-ups and redirects to unwanted websites. These pop-ups can appear even when your web browser is not open, indicating that the malware is deeply embedded in your system. While legitimate websites sometimes display ads, a sudden increase in the number of intrusive or irrelevant ads is a red flag. Additionally, these pop-ups may prompt you to download dubious software or reveal personal information, further compromising your security.

Frequent system crashes and error messages can also signal a malware infection. If your computer crashes unexpectedly or displays error messages regularly, it could be due to malware interfering with critical system processes. Malware often targets system files and applications, causing instability and errors. These crashes can result in data loss and disrupt your workflow. Paying attention to the frequency and timing of these crashes can help determine if malware is the root cause.

Another telltale sign of a malware infection is the appearance of unfamiliar programs or files on your computer. Malware can install additional malicious software without your consent, leading to the presence of unknown applications or files. These programs may run automatically at startup, further slowing down your system. If you notice new icons on your desktop or new entries in your task manager or system tray that you did not install, it is essential to investigate their origin. Legitimate software typically prompts for installation and requires user consent, whereas malware operates covertly.

Changes to your web browser's behavior can also indicate a malware infection. If your browser's homepage or search engine is suddenly different, or if you are frequently redirected to suspicious websites, malware may be at work. Browser hijackers, a form of malware, alter browser settings to redirect traffic to specific sites, often for advertising revenue or to spread additional malware. These changes can be challenging to reverse, as the malware may reinstall itself or restore its settings after a reboot.

Unexplained disk activity is another symptom of malware. If you notice that your hard drive is constantly active, even when you are not using your computer, it could be due to malware performing background tasks. This activity can include writing and reading data, scanning for personal information, or communicating with a remote server. Monitoring your system's disk activity through task manager or activity monitor can help identify unusual patterns that may indicate malware presence.

A sudden increase in network activity can also be a sign of a malware infection. Malware often communicates with remote servers to exfiltrate data, receive commands, or download additional payloads. If your internet connection is slower than usual, or if you notice unexplained spikes in data usage, it could be due to malware transmitting data in the background. Using network monitoring tools can help detect unusual traffic patterns and identify potential threats.

Another concerning sign of malware is the appearance of security warnings from your antivirus software or firewall. If your security software alerts you to a potential threat, it is crucial to take these warnings seriously. Some advanced malware can disable or bypass security software, so frequent or unusual alerts should not be ignored. In some cases, malware may prevent your antivirus software from running or updating, indicating a severe infection that requires immediate attention.

Ransomware infections have a very distinct and alarming symptom: the encryption of your files accompanied by a ransom demand. If you suddenly find that you cannot access your files and see a message demanding payment to restore access, your computer is likely infected with ransomware. This type of malware encrypts personal or organizational data and demands payment for the decryption key. It is essential to avoid paying the ransom, as there is no guarantee that the attackers will provide the key, and it encourages further criminal activity. Instead, seek professional assistance to address the infection.

Spyware infections, while more covert, can be detected through signs such as unusual behavior in your accounts, unauthorized financial transactions, or the appearance of unknown devices connected to your online accounts. Spyware monitors and collects information about your activities, often leading to identity theft or financial fraud. Regularly reviewing account activity and being vigilant about any unauthorized access can help detect spyware infections early.

In conclusion, recognizing the signs of a malware infection is vital for maintaining the security and functionality of your computer systems. Symptoms such as decreased system performance, unexpected pop-up ads, frequent crashes, unfamiliar programs, changes in browser behavior, unexplained disk and network activity, security warnings, and the encryption of files all indicate potential malware presence.

By staying vigilant and responding promptly to these signs, users can mitigate the impact of malware and protect their data. Regularly updating software, using reputable security tools, and practicing safe browsing and email habits are essential steps in preventing and detecting malware infections.

Understanding these indicators enables users to take proactive measures, ensuring a secure and efficient digital environment.

Chapter 5: The Importance of Regular Software Updates

In the digital age, software is the backbone of nearly every aspect of our daily lives, from personal communications and entertainment to business operations and critical infrastructure. Regular software updates are crucial for maintaining the security, functionality, and efficiency of these systems. Despite their importance, updates are often neglected or postponed by users who may find them inconvenient or disruptive. Understanding the significance of these updates can help highlight why they should be a priority.

One of the primary reasons for regular software updates is security. Cyber threats are continually evolving, with hackers and malicious entities developing new methods to exploit vulnerabilities in software. These vulnerabilities are weaknesses or flaws in the code that can be exploited to gain unauthorized access to systems, steal data, or cause damage. Software developers constantly monitor their products for such vulnerabilities and release updates, often referred to as patches, to fix them. By applying these patches promptly, users can protect their systems from being compromised by newly discovered threats.

In addition to addressing vulnerabilities, software updates also include enhancements that bolster the overall security of applications and operating systems. These enhancements might involve the introduction of new security features, improvements to existing ones, or modifications to the software's architecture to make it more resilient against attacks. Regular updates ensure that users benefit from the latest advancements in cybersecurity, making it more difficult for attackers to breach their defenses.

Beyond security, updates are essential for maintaining the functionality and performance of software. Over time, as technology advances and new hardware components are developed, software needs to be updated to remain compatible and efficient. Updates can include performance optimizations that enhance the speed and responsiveness of applications, ensuring they run smoothly on the latest hardware and operating systems. Without these updates, software can become sluggish, unresponsive, or incompatible with newer systems, leading to a degraded user experience.

Software updates also play a critical role in fixing bugs and other issues that can affect the usability and reliability of applications. Bugs are errors or flaws in the software code that can cause programs to behave unexpectedly or crash. While developers strive to release stable and error-free software, it is nearly impossible to anticipate every possible scenario in which the software might be used. As users report issues and developers identify bugs, updates are released to address these problems. By keeping software up to date, users can avoid many of the frustrations and disruptions caused by bugs.

Another important aspect of software updates is the introduction of new features and functionalities. The software development landscape is highly competitive, and developers continually seek to improve their products to meet user demands and stay ahead of the competition. Updates often bring new features that enhance the capabilities of applications, providing users with new tools and functionalities that can improve their productivity, creativity, and overall experience. Regular updates ensure that users have access to the latest innovations and improvements, allowing them to take full advantage of their software.

Compliance with regulatory requirements is another reason why regular software updates are important. In many industries, there are strict regulations governing data protection, privacy, and security. Software that processes or stores sensitive information must comply with these regulations to avoid legal penalties and protect users' data. Regulatory bodies frequently update their requirements to address emerging threats and changes in technology. Software updates ensure that applications remain compliant with the latest regulations, helping organizations avoid fines and legal issues while protecting their users' data.

The interconnected nature of modern software ecosystems further underscores the importance of updates. Many applications and services rely on third-party libraries, frameworks, and APIs to function. These dependencies are also subject to updates, and failing to keep them current can introduce vulnerabilities or compatibility issues. Regular updates ensure that all components of the software ecosystem are synchronized and functioning correctly, reducing the risk of conflicts and security breaches.

For businesses and organizations, the cost of not updating software can be substantial. Security breaches resulting from unpatched vulnerabilities can lead to data loss, financial losses, and damage to reputation. Recovering from a cyber attack can be costly and time-consuming, involving forensic investigations, legal fees, and the implementation of additional security measures. Regular updates are a proactive measure that can significantly reduce the risk of such incidents, protecting the organization's assets and reputation.

Despite the clear benefits of regular software updates, many users are hesitant to apply them. Common reasons include concerns about compatibility issues, fear of data loss, and the perceived inconvenience of the update process. While these concerns are understandable, they can be mitigated through proper planning and best practices. For example, users can schedule updates during off-peak hours to minimize disruption, back up their data before applying updates to prevent data loss, and test updates in a controlled environment to identify potential compatibility issues.

Automated update mechanisms can also simplify the process and ensure that updates are applied promptly. Most modern software and operating systems offer options for automatic updates, reducing the burden on users to manually check for and install updates. By enabling automatic updates, users can ensure that their software remains current with minimal effort, allowing them to focus on their tasks without worrying about security and performance issues.

In conclusion, regular software updates are a fundamental aspect of maintaining the security, functionality, and efficiency of modern software. They protect against evolving cyber threats, enhance performance, fix bugs, introduce new features, ensure regulatory compliance, and

maintain compatibility within the software
ecosystem.

While the update process may seem inconvenient,
the benefits far outweigh the potential risks and
costs of neglecting updates. By prioritizing regular
updates and adopting best practices for their
implementation, users can safeguard their digital
environments and enjoy a more secure, reliable,
and feature-rich software experience.

Understanding the importance of updates is the
first step towards a proactive approach to software
maintenance, ultimately leading to a safer and
more efficient digital world.

Chapter 6: Choosing and Using Antivirus Software

In today's interconnected digital world, where cyber threats lurk around every corner of the internet, protecting your devices from malicious software has become a paramount concern. Antivirus software plays a crucial role in safeguarding your computer and personal information from viruses, malware, ransomware, and other harmful programs that can wreak havoc on your system. However, not all antivirus solutions are created equal, and choosing the right one requires careful consideration of several key factors.

Understanding Antivirus Software

Before delving into what to look for in antivirus software, it's essential to understand its primary function. Antivirus software is designed to detect, prevent, and remove malicious software from your computer or device. It works by scanning files and programs for known patterns of harmful behavior or code signatures. Modern antivirus solutions also employ heuristic analysis and behavior-based detection to identify new threats that may not yet have known signatures.

Key Features to Consider

When selecting antivirus software, the range of features offered can greatly impact its effectiveness in protecting your system. Here are some essential features to consider:

1. Real-Time Protection: This feature actively monitors your computer in real-time, scanning files as they are accessed or downloaded. It ensures immediate detection and blocking of threats before they can cause harm.

2. Malware Detection and Removal: Effective antivirus software should have a high detection rate for various types of malware, including viruses, Trojans, spyware, adware, and ransomware. It should also be capable of completely removing detected threats from your system.

3. System Performance Impact: Antivirus software should operate efficiently without significantly slowing down your computer's performance. Look for solutions that are optimized to minimize resource usage during scans and real-time protection.

4. Ease of Use and User Interface: A user-friendly interface is important for managing scans, viewing security status, and accessing additional features.

Intuitive controls and clear, actionable alerts contribute to a positive user experience.

5. Compatibility: Ensure that the antivirus software is compatible with your operating system and other software applications you use. Some solutions offer cross-platform protection for multiple devices, including PCs, Macs, smartphones, and tablets.

6. Additional Security Tools: Many antivirus packages include supplementary tools such as firewalls, email scanners, browser protection, and parental controls. Evaluate these extras based on your specific security needs.

Choosing the Right Antivirus Software

With a myriad of antivirus solutions available, selecting the right one can be daunting. Here are steps to help you make an informed decision:

1. Assess Your Needs: Consider the specific threats you're concerned about and the devices you need to protect. For instance, if you primarily use a Mac, look for antivirus software tailored for macOS.

2. Research and Comparison: Read reviews and independent test results from reputable sources to evaluate the effectiveness and reliability of different antivirus products. Pay attention to factors like detection rates, false positive rates, and impact on system performance.

3. Trial Versions and Testing: Take advantage of free trial versions offered by antivirus vendors to test the software's features and performance on your system. Use this opportunity to assess ease of installation, usability, and overall satisfaction with the product.

4. Consider Paid vs. Free Solutions: While free antivirus software can provide basic protection, paid solutions often offer more comprehensive features, including customer support, frequent updates, and advanced threat detection capabilities.

5. Reputation and Support: Choose a well-established antivirus vendor with a strong reputation for timely updates and responsive customer support. Look for software that offers regular updates to protect against emerging threats.

Implementing Antivirus Best Practices

Once you've selected and installed antivirus software, implementing best practices will further enhance your cybersecurity:

1. Keep Software Updated: Regularly update your antivirus software to ensure it can detect and protect against the latest threats. Enable automatic updates whenever possible to stay protected against emerging vulnerabilities.

2. Perform Regular Scans: Schedule regular scans of your system to detect and remove any potential threats that may have evaded real-time protection. Full system scans can help identify hidden malware and ensure comprehensive security.

3. Exercise Caution Online: Practice safe browsing habits and avoid clicking on suspicious links or downloading files from untrusted sources. Be cautious of phishing emails and scams designed to trick you into revealing sensitive information.

4. Backup Important Data: Regularly back up your important files and data to an external hard drive or cloud storage service. In the event of a malware infection or system compromise, backups will allow you to restore your files without paying ransom or losing valuable information.

Conclusion

Choosing and using antivirus software is a critical aspect of maintaining cybersecurity in today's digital landscape. By understanding the key features to look for, conducting thorough research, and implementing best practices, you can effectively protect your devices from a wide range of online threats.

Remember, proactive measures and informed decisions are key to safeguarding your digital assets and ensuring peace of mind in an increasingly interconnected world.

Chapter 7: The Role of Firewalls in Malware Protection

In the ever-evolving landscape of cybersecurity threats, firewalls stand as stalwart guardians, playing a crucial role in defending against malware and unauthorized access to computer networks. Understanding how firewalls contribute to malware protection is essential for both individual users and organizations striving to safeguard sensitive data and maintain operational integrity.

Understanding Firewalls

A firewall is a network security system that acts as a barrier between a trusted internal network and untrusted external networks, such as the internet. Its primary function is to monitor and control incoming and outgoing network traffic based on predetermined security rules. By enforcing these rules, firewalls help prevent unauthorized access to or from private networks while allowing legitimate communication to proceed.

Types of Firewalls

Firewalls can be categorized into several types based on their operational characteristics and deployment:

1. **Packet Filtering Firewalls:** These are the most basic type of firewalls and operate at the network layer (Layer 3) of the OSI model. Packet filtering firewalls examine each packet of data as it passes through the network and either blocks or allows it based on predefined rules, such as source IP address, destination IP address, port numbers, and protocol type.
2. **Stateful Inspection Firewalls:** Also known as dynamic packet filtering firewalls, these operate at both the network layer and transport layer (Layer 4). Stateful inspection firewalls keep track of the state of network connections and use this information to determine whether to allow or block traffic. This method offers more advanced protection compared to packet filtering firewalls by considering the context of each packet.
3. **Proxy Firewalls:** Proxy firewalls act as intermediaries between internal and external systems. They intercept incoming and outgoing traffic and forward it on behalf of the client. By doing so, proxy firewalls can provide additional security features, such as content filtering and application-layer filtering, which inspect the actual content of packets for malicious code or unauthorized content.

4. **Next-Generation Firewalls (NGFW):** NGFWs integrate traditional firewall functionalities with additional features such as intrusion prevention systems (IPS), application awareness, and deep packet inspection. These advanced capabilities enable NGFWs to identify and block sophisticated threats, including certain types of malware that may attempt to exploit application vulnerabilities or use advanced evasion techniques.

Role of Firewalls in Malware Protection

Firewalls play a critical role in defending against malware by implementing several key strategies:

1. **Blocking Known Malicious Traffic:** Firewalls can be configured to block incoming and outgoing traffic that matches known patterns of malicious behavior or signatures associated with malware. This proactive approach helps prevent malware infections by denying access to infected websites, malicious servers, or communication channels used by malware to spread.
2. **Monitoring and Filtering Outbound Traffic:** In addition to blocking incoming threats, firewalls monitor outbound traffic to detect signs of malware infections within the network. By analyzing outbound communication patterns and inspecting data

packets for suspicious content, firewalls can identify compromised devices attempting to communicate with command-and-control servers or transmit sensitive information.

3. **Preventing Unauthorized Access:** Firewalls act as a barrier against unauthorized access attempts, including remote exploitation attempts by malware-infected systems. By enforcing access control policies and filtering traffic based on source IP addresses, port numbers, and application protocols, firewalls reduce the risk of external attackers gaining unauthorized access to internal networks or sensitive data.

4. **Detecting Anomalies and Intrusions:** Advanced firewalls, such as NGFWs and those equipped with intrusion detection and prevention capabilities, actively monitor network traffic for anomalies indicative of malware activity or potential intrusion attempts. By correlating network events and applying behavioral analysis techniques, these firewalls can detect suspicious behaviors that may indicate the presence of malware or unauthorized access attempts.

5. **Enhancing Network Segmentation:** Firewalls facilitate network segmentation by dividing a network into distinct security zones or segments with different levels of trust. By placing firewalls between segments and

enforcing strict access controls, organizations can contain malware outbreaks and limit the lateral movement of threats within their network infrastructure.

Best Practices for Firewall Configuration and Management

To maximize the effectiveness of firewalls in malware protection, organizations and individuals should adhere to best practices for firewall configuration and management:

- **Define Clear Security Policies:** Establish comprehensive firewall security policies that align with organizational security objectives and regulatory compliance requirements. Clearly define rules for allowed and blocked traffic based on the principle of least privilege.
- **Regularly Update Firewall Rules:** Maintain up-to-date firewall rules and access control lists (ACLs) to reflect changes in network topology, application requirements, and emerging threats. Periodically review and audit firewall configurations to ensure they remain effective against evolving malware threats.
- **Implement Multi-Layered Defense:** Combine firewall protection with other security measures, such as antivirus software,

intrusion detection systems (IDS), and security information and event management (SIEM) solutions, to create a multi-layered defense strategy. This approach enhances overall cybersecurity resilience and reduces reliance on any single security control.

- **Monitor Firewall Logs and Alerts:** Actively monitor firewall logs and alerts for signs of suspicious activity, such as repeated connection attempts from unrecognized IP addresses or unusual traffic patterns. Implement automated alerting mechanisms to promptly notify security teams of potential malware incidents or policy violations.

- **Regularly Conduct Security Assessments:** Perform regular vulnerability assessments and penetration testing to identify weaknesses in firewall configurations and network defenses. Use the findings to remediate security gaps and strengthen overall malware protection capabilities.

Conclusion

In conclusion, firewalls serve as essential components of a robust cybersecurity posture, playing a pivotal role in protecting against malware and unauthorized access to networks.

By implementing firewalls with appropriate configurations, regularly updating security policies, and integrating them with complementary security technologies, organizations and individuals can effectively mitigate the risks posed by malware and maintain the confidentiality, integrity, and availability of critical assets and information.

Embracing proactive security measures and staying informed about emerging threats will further enhance the effectiveness of firewalls in safeguarding against the evolving landscape of cybersecurity threats.

Chapter 8: Safe Browsing Practices to Avoid Malware

In today's digital age, the internet serves as a gateway to vast resources, entertainment, and communication platforms. However, alongside its benefits, the internet also harbors numerous threats, including malware—malicious software designed to infiltrate, damage, or gain unauthorized access to computer systems. Safeguarding against malware begins with adopting safe browsing practices. Whether you're browsing for work, leisure, or research, understanding and implementing these practices can significantly reduce the risk of encountering malware and protect your personal information.

Understanding Malware and Its Risks

Malware encompasses a broad spectrum of malicious software, including viruses, Trojans, spyware, ransomware, adware, and phishing attacks. Each type of malware operates differently but shares the common goal of exploiting vulnerabilities in systems or user behaviors to compromise security. The consequences of malware infections range from data theft and financial loss to system instability and unauthorized access to sensitive information.

Essential Safe Browsing Practices

1. **Keep Software Updated:** Ensure your operating system, web browsers, plugins, and applications are regularly updated with the latest security patches and updates. Software updates often include fixes for known vulnerabilities that malware may exploit to infiltrate your system.

2. **Use Secure Connections:** When browsing the web, especially when entering sensitive information such as passwords or financial details, ensure the website uses HTTPS (Hypertext Transfer Protocol Secure). HTTPS encrypts data transmitted between your browser and the website, protecting it from interception by malicious actors.

3. **Verify Website Authenticity:** Be cautious of phishing websites that mimic legitimate sites to steal login credentials or distribute malware. Verify the authenticity of websites by checking the URL for typos or suspicious variations, and look for HTTPS encryption, a padlock icon, or security indicators in the browser's address bar.

4. **Exercise Caution with Email Links and Attachments:** Avoid clicking on links or downloading attachments from unsolicited or suspicious emails, even if they appear to be from trusted sources. Malware often spreads through phishing emails that entice

recipients to click on malicious links or
download infected files.

5. **Enable Pop-Up Blockers:** Configure your
    web browser to block pop-up windows, as
    they can potentially contain malicious
    content or redirect you to phishing websites.
    Most modern web browsers offer built-in
    pop-up blockers that can be enabled through
    browser settings.

6. **Use Ad Blockers:** Consider using ad-blocking
    extensions or plugins in your web browser to
    reduce exposure to malicious
    advertisements (malvertising) that may
    redirect you to compromised websites or
    attempt to download malware onto your
    device.

7. **Be Mindful of Downloads:** Download
    software, files, and media content only from
    reputable sources and official websites.
    Avoid downloading pirated or cracked
    software, as these often contain hidden
    malware or unwanted programs bundled
    with the download.

8. **Employ Web Filtering Tools:** Utilize web
    filtering tools or parental control software to
    block access to potentially malicious or
    inappropriate websites, particularly on
    devices used by children or in corporate
    environments to enforce security policies.

9. **Backup Important Data:** Regularly back up
    your important files and data to an external

hard drive, cloud storage service, or backup solution. In the event of a malware infection or ransomware attack, backups enable you to restore your data without paying ransom or losing critical information.

10. **Educate Yourself and Others:** Stay informed about the latest cybersecurity threats and educate yourself and others about safe browsing practices. Encourage family members, colleagues, and employees to follow cybersecurity best practices to collectively reduce the risk of malware infections.

Implementing Safe Browsing Practices

Implementing safe browsing practices requires a combination of awareness, vigilance, and proactive measures to mitigate the risks posed by malware:

- **Stay Vigilant:** Remain cautious and skeptical of unfamiliar websites, links, emails, and online advertisements. Exercise discretion when sharing personal information online and avoid oversharing on social media platforms.
- **Use Strong, Unique Passwords:** Create strong passwords consisting of a mix of letters, numbers, and special characters for online accounts. Avoid using easily guessable passwords or reusing passwords

across multiple websites to prevent unauthorized access in case of a data breach.

- **Enable Two-Factor Authentication (2FA):** Enhance the security of your online accounts by enabling two-factor authentication wherever possible. 2FA adds an additional layer of verification beyond passwords, reducing the risk of unauthorized access even if your password is compromised.
- **Regularly Scan for Malware:** Use reputable antivirus software to regularly scan your devices for malware and other security threats. Ensure the antivirus software is updated with the latest virus definitions to detect and remove emerging threats effectively.

Conclusion

By adopting and consistently practicing safe browsing habits, individuals and organizations can minimize the risk of encountering malware and protect their sensitive information and digital assets. Safe browsing practices not only safeguard against malware infections but also contribute to a safer and more secure online experience.

Embrace these practices as part of your daily routine to fortify your defenses against the evolving landscape of cybersecurity threats and enjoy a safer browsing experience across the internet.

Chapter 9: Avoiding Phishing Scams

In the realm of cybersecurity threats, phishing scams continue to pose a significant risk to individuals and organizations alike. Phishing is a deceptive technique used by cybercriminals to trick users into divulging sensitive information, such as login credentials, financial details, or personal data. These scams often masquerade as legitimate communications from trusted entities, including banks, social media platforms, government agencies, and online services. Understanding how phishing scams operate and adopting proactive measures to recognize and avoid them are crucial steps in safeguarding against identity theft, financial fraud, and other malicious activities facilitated by phishing.

Understanding Phishing Scams

Phishing scams typically involve fraudulent emails, text messages, or websites designed to deceive recipients into taking actions that benefit the attacker. Common characteristics of phishing scams include:

- **Impersonation of Trusted Sources:** Attackers impersonate legitimate organizations or individuals familiar to the recipient, such as banks, government agencies, online retailers, or colleagues, to establish credibility and gain trust.

- **Urgency and Fear Tactics:** Phishing messages often create a sense of urgency or fear to prompt immediate action from the recipient, such as threatening account closure, fines, or legal consequences if sensitive information is not provided promptly.
- **Spoofed Communication Channels:** Attackers may spoof email addresses, phone numbers, or website URLs to mimic legitimate sources, making it challenging for recipients to distinguish between genuine and fraudulent communications.
- **Requests for Sensitive Information:** Phishing scams commonly request recipients to provide sensitive information, such as usernames, passwords, social security numbers, credit card details, or answers to security questions, under false pretenses.

Recognizing Phishing Attempts

Recognizing phishing attempts requires vigilance and awareness of common tactics used by cybercriminals to deceive individuals:

- **Check the Sender's Email Address:** Examine the sender's email address carefully for discrepancies or slight variations from legitimate addresses. Attackers often use domain names resembling trusted organizations but with minor alterations or misspellings.

- **Verify Message Content:** Scrutinize the content of emails, text messages, or websites for grammatical errors, spelling mistakes, or unusual language that may indicate a phishing attempt. Legitimate communications from reputable sources typically maintain a high standard of professionalism and accuracy.
- **Assess Links and URLs:** Hover your mouse cursor over hyperlinks embedded in emails or messages to reveal the destination URL. Be cautious of URLs that redirect to unfamiliar or suspicious websites unrelated to the purported sender's domain.
- **Avoid Unsolicited Attachments:** Refrain from downloading attachments or clicking on links in unsolicited emails or messages, especially from unknown senders or sources. Malicious attachments can contain malware designed to compromise your device or steal sensitive information.
- **Verify Requests for Information:** Exercise caution when asked to provide sensitive information or login credentials via email, text message, or online form. Verify the legitimacy of requests by contacting the

organization directly through official channels before sharing any personal data.

Best Practices for Avoiding Phishing Scams

Implementing proactive measures and best practices can help mitigate the risk of falling victim to phishing scams:

- **Educate and Train Users:** Educate yourself and others about phishing tactics and the importance of cybersecurity awareness. Conduct regular training sessions or workshops to familiarize employees, family members, and colleagues with phishing prevention strategies and techniques for recognizing suspicious communications.
- **Use Security Tools and Technologies:** Employ spam filters, email authentication protocols (e.g., SPF, DKIM, DMARC), and advanced threat detection solutions to identify and block phishing emails before they reach recipients' inboxes. These technologies help mitigate the risk of exposure to malicious content and phishing attempts.
- **Enable Multi-Factor Authentication (MFA):** Enable MFA on online accounts and services to add an extra layer of security beyond passwords. MFA requires users to provide additional verification, such as a code sent

to their mobile device, before accessing their accounts, reducing the likelihood of unauthorized access in the event of credential theft.

- **Keep Software Updated:** Regularly update your operating system, web browsers, antivirus software, and other applications with the latest security patches and updates. Software updates often include fixes for vulnerabilities exploited by phishing attacks and other cyber threats.
- **Monitor Financial Accounts:** Regularly monitor your bank statements, credit card transactions, and financial accounts for unauthorized or suspicious activity. Report any discrepancies or unauthorized transactions to your financial institution promptly to minimize potential losses due to phishing-related fraud.
- **Report and Block Phishing Attempts:** Report suspected phishing emails, text messages, or websites to the appropriate authorities, such as your email service provider, IT department, or cybersecurity agency. Blocking senders or domains associated with phishing attempts helps prevent future exposure to similar scams.

Conclusion

Phishing scams continue to evolve in sophistication and frequency, posing a persistent threat to individuals, businesses, and organizations worldwide. By understanding the tactics used by cybercriminals, recognizing common indicators of phishing attempts, and adopting proactive security measures, you can significantly reduce the risk of falling victim to phishing scams.

Vigilance, skepticism, and a commitment to cybersecurity awareness empower individuals to protect their sensitive information, financial assets, and digital identities from the detrimental effects of phishing and other forms of cybercrime.

Chapter 10: The Importance of Strong, Unique Passwords

In today's digital age, where virtually every aspect of our lives is interconnected through online accounts and services, the importance of strong, unique passwords cannot be overstated. Passwords serve as the first line of defense against unauthorized access to sensitive information, personal data, financial assets, and digital identities. However, many individuals underestimate the significance of password security, often opting for convenience over robust protection. Understanding why strong, unique passwords are crucial and implementing best practices for password management are essential steps in safeguarding against cyber threats and maintaining privacy and security online.

Understanding Password Security

Passwords are strings of characters—typically a combination of letters, numbers, and symbols—that authenticate and grant access to user accounts, devices, or systems. They serve as a fundamental security measure, verifying the identity of authorized users and restricting access to unauthorized individuals or malicious actors. Weak or compromised passwords are susceptible to brute-force attacks, dictionary attacks, and password guessing techniques employed by cybercriminals to gain unauthorized access to accounts or sensitive information.

Characteristics of Strong Passwords

Strong passwords possess several characteristics that enhance their effectiveness in protecting accounts from unauthorized access:

- **Length:** Longer passwords are generally more secure than shorter ones, as they increase the complexity and difficulty of guessing or cracking through automated attacks. Experts recommend using passwords with a minimum of 12 characters or more.
- **Complexity:** Incorporating a mix of uppercase letters, lowercase letters, numbers, and special symbols (e.g., !, @, #, $) increases the complexity of passwords, making them more resistant to brute-force attacks and password cracking tools.
- **Unpredictability:** Avoid using easily guessable information, such as common words, phrases, or predictable patterns (e.g., "password123," "qwerty," or sequential numbers). Instead, create passwords that are random, unique, and difficult for others to guess.

- **Avoiding Personal Information:** Refrain from using personal information such as names, birthdates, addresses, or family members' names in passwords. Attackers may exploit publicly available information or social engineering techniques to guess passwords based on personal details.

Risks of Weak Passwords

Weak passwords pose significant security risks and vulnerabilities that can compromise the integrity and confidentiality of sensitive information:

- **Account Compromise:** Cybercriminals can exploit weak passwords to gain unauthorized access to user accounts, allowing them to steal personal data, financial information, or sensitive corporate information.
- **Identity Theft:** Compromised passwords facilitate identity theft, enabling attackers to impersonate victims online, conduct fraudulent transactions, or access confidential resources associated with compromised accounts.
- **Data Breaches:** Inadequate password security contributes to data breaches, where large-scale unauthorized access to sensitive information occurs due to weak or reused

passwords across multiple accounts or services.

- **Reputational Damage:** Organizations and individuals may suffer reputational damage and loss of trust from customers, clients, or stakeholders in the event of a security breach resulting from weak password practices.

Best Practices for Password Management

Implementing effective password management practices enhances security and reduces the risk of unauthorized access or data breaches:

- **Use Unique Passwords for Each Account:** Avoid using the same password across multiple accounts or services. Use a unique password for each account to prevent a single password compromise from affecting multiple accounts.
- **Password Complexity and Length:** Create strong passwords by incorporating a combination of uppercase letters, lowercase letters, numbers, and special symbols. Aim for passwords that are at least 12 characters long to increase complexity and resilience against attacks.
- **Consider Password Managers:** Use reputable password management tools or password managers to generate, store, and

securely manage complex passwords for multiple accounts. Password managers encrypt and store passwords in a secure vault, requiring a master password for access.

- **Enable Multi-Factor Authentication (MFA):** Enable MFA or two-factor authentication (2FA) wherever possible to add an extra layer of security beyond passwords. MFA requires users to provide additional verification, such as a code sent to their mobile device, to access accounts, reducing the risk of unauthorized access in case of password compromise.
- **Regularly Update Passwords:** Periodically change passwords for sensitive accounts or services, especially after a security incident or data breach. Avoid reusing previous passwords and ensure new passwords meet current security standards for complexity and length.
- **Secure Password Storage:** Avoid storing passwords in plaintext or insecure locations, such as unencrypted text files, emails, or notes. Use encrypted storage solutions or password managers to protect sensitive information from unauthorized access.
- **Educate and Raise Awareness:** Educate employees, colleagues, friends, and family members about the importance of password security and best practices for creating and

managing strong passwords. Encourage the adoption of secure password practices to collectively strengthen cybersecurity defenses.

Conclusion

Strong, unique passwords are fundamental to maintaining cybersecurity and protecting personal information, financial assets, and digital identities from unauthorized access and cyber threats.

By understanding the characteristics of strong passwords, recognizing the risks associated with weak passwords, and implementing best practices for password management, individuals and organizations can enhance their resilience against evolving cybersecurity threats.

Embrace password security as a proactive measure to safeguard sensitive information and maintain trust and confidence in an increasingly interconnected digital world.

Chapter 11: Multi-Factor Authentication: An Extra Layer of Security

In the ever-evolving landscape of cybersecurity, where threats lurk around every digital corner, the importance of robust authentication mechanisms cannot be overstated. As organizations and individuals alike strive to safeguard sensitive information from malicious actors, multi-factor authentication (MFA) emerges as a beacon of hope—a reliable extra layer of security that fortifies access controls beyond the traditional username and password paradigm.

Understanding Multi-Factor Authentication

At its core, multi-factor authentication enhances security by requiring users to provide multiple forms of verification to gain access to a system or account. This approach acknowledges the inherent vulnerabilities of single-factor authentication, where compromise of a password alone could lead to unauthorized access. By demanding additional factors beyond something the user knows (typically a password), MFA significantly bolsters defense mechanisms against unauthorized access attempts.

The Three Factors of Authentication

Authentication factors typically fall into three categories: something the user knows, something the user has, and something the user is.

1. Knowledge Factors: The most common knowledge factor is the password or passphrase—a string of characters known only to the user. However, passwords alone have proven insufficient against sophisticated cyberattacks such as brute-force attacks or phishing schemes. To mitigate these risks, organizations often enforce password complexity requirements and encourage the use of passphrases—a longer sequence of words that are easier to remember yet harder to crack.

2. Possession Factors: Possession factors involve something tangible that the user possesses, such as a physical token or a mobile device. These tokens generate time-based or event-based codes that users must enter alongside their passwords during login attempts. Alternatively, some implementations utilize push notifications sent to a registered device, requiring user confirmation to proceed with authentication. This method not only validates the user's identity but also ensures the possession of a specific device linked to the account.

3. Inherence Factors: Inherence factors leverage unique biological or behavioral traits of the user, such as fingerprints, facial recognition, voice patterns, or keystroke dynamics. These factors are increasingly integrated into authentication systems, particularly on mobile devices equipped with biometric sensors. Biometric authentication offers a seamless user experience while enhancing security through the verification of physical or behavioral traits that are difficult to replicate.

Advantages of Multi-Factor Authentication

The adoption of MFA brings several compelling advantages to both individuals and organizations navigating today's digital environment:

1. Enhanced Security Posture: By requiring multiple factors for authentication, MFA mitigates the risk of unauthorized access resulting from compromised passwords. Even if an attacker manages to obtain a user's password, additional authentication factors serve as barriers, significantly raising the complexity of a successful breach.

2. Compliance Requirements: Many industries and regulatory bodies mandate the use of MFA as part of their cybersecurity frameworks. Compliance with these standards not only helps organizations avoid penalties but also demonstrates a commitment to safeguarding sensitive data and maintaining customer trust.

3. User Convenience: Contrary to popular belief, MFA implementations can enhance user convenience when thoughtfully designed. Methods such as biometric authentication or push notifications reduce the cognitive load associated with remembering complex passwords without compromising security.

4. Scalability and Adaptability: MFA solutions are scalable across various platforms and adaptable to different user needs and preferences. Whether deployed in enterprise environments, consumer applications, or governmental systems, MFA frameworks can accommodate diverse authentication methods without sacrificing security or usability.

Implementing Multi-Factor Authentication

Effective implementation of MFA requires careful consideration of organizational needs, user experience, and technical feasibility. Key steps in deploying MFA include:

1. Risk Assessment: Begin with a comprehensive assessment of organizational risks and threats. Identify critical systems, sensitive data, and potential vulnerabilities that MFA could help mitigate.

2. Selecting Authentication Methods: Evaluate available authentication methods based on usability, security strength, and compatibility with existing systems. Consider factors such as user demographics, device types, and regulatory requirements when choosing appropriate MFA solutions.

3. User Education and Awareness: Educate users about the benefits of MFA, proper authentication practices, and potential phishing tactics targeting multi-factor authentication. Encourage users to enable MFA on all applicable accounts and provide clear instructions on how to set up and use MFA effectively.

4. Monitoring and Continuous Improvement: Implement monitoring mechanisms to detect anomalies or unauthorized access attempts. Regularly review MFA policies and procedures to incorporate emerging threats and technological advancements into the authentication framework.

Challenges and Considerations

Despite its clear benefits, implementing MFA poses several challenges that organizations must address:

1. Usability Concerns: Poorly implemented MFA solutions can frustrate users, leading to resistance or non-compliance. Organizations should prioritize user experience by selecting intuitive authentication methods and providing adequate support and training.

2. Integration Complexity: Integrating MFA with existing systems and applications can be complex, particularly in heterogeneous IT environments. Consideration should be given to interoperability, scalability, and potential impacts on system performance during integration efforts.

3. Cost Implications: While the cost of MFA solutions varies, organizations must weigh the financial implications against potential security benefits. Cost-effective strategies include leveraging cloud-based authentication services or adopting open-source authentication frameworks.

Future Trends in Multi-Factor Authentication

Looking ahead, several trends are poised to shape the future of MFA:

1. Passwordless Authentication: Emerging technologies such as WebAuthn and FIDO2 are paving the way for passwordless authentication methods that rely on cryptographic protocols and biometric factors. These advancements promise to streamline user authentication while enhancing security and user experience.

2. Behavioral Biometrics: Advancements in artificial intelligence and machine learning are enhancing the accuracy and reliability of behavioral biometrics, which analyze unique patterns in user behavior (e.g., typing speed, mouse movements) to authenticate identity. These methods offer continuous authentication capabilities, further strengthening security without compromising user convenience.

3. Zero Trust Security Frameworks: The adoption of zero trust security principles, which assume breach and verify every request as though it originates from an open network, aligns closely with the principles of MFA. By combining MFA with continuous monitoring and least privilege access controls, organizations can establish a robust security posture against evolving threats.

Conclusion

In conclusion, multi-factor authentication stands as a cornerstone of modern cybersecurity strategies, offering an indispensable layer of defense against unauthorized access and data breaches.

By leveraging multiple authentication factors—knowledge, possession, and inherence—

organizations can fortify their defenses while enhancing user experience and regulatory compliance.

As technological advancements continue to reshape the cybersecurity landscape, the evolution of MFA promises to play a pivotal role in safeguarding digital identities and securing sensitive information in an increasingly interconnected world.

Chapter 12: The Risks of Downloading Free Software

In today's digital age, the allure of free software is undeniable. From productivity tools to multimedia applications and antivirus programs, a plethora of free software offerings promise to enhance user experience without costing a dime. However, beneath the surface of this apparent generosity lurk significant risks and potential pitfalls that users must navigate cautiously. This chapter delves into the multifaceted risks associated with downloading free software, shedding light on the implications for security, privacy, and overall digital well-being.

Understanding Free Software: The Appeal and Perils

Free software, often distributed under open-source licenses or as freeware, appeals to users seeking cost-effective solutions for various computing needs. Whether developed by enthusiasts, community-driven projects, or established companies offering "lite" versions of premium software, free applications promise functionality without the financial commitment. This accessibility has democratized access to software tools, empowering users globally. However, the adage "there's no such thing as a free lunch" rings particularly true in the realm of free software, where hidden costs and risks may overshadow the initial appeal.

Security Risks: Malware, Adware, and Potentially Unwanted Programs (PUPs)

One of the foremost concerns associated with free software is the heightened risk of encountering malware, adware, or potentially unwanted programs (PUPs). Unlike commercial software subjected to rigorous testing and security audits, free applications may lack robust quality assurance processes, making them vulnerable to exploitation by malicious actors. Malware disguised as legitimate software can infiltrate systems, compromising data integrity, and exposing users to identity theft, financial fraud, or unauthorized access.

Moreover, some free software packages are bundled with adware—a type of software that displays intrusive advertisements or collects user data for targeted marketing purposes. While not inherently malicious, adware can degrade system performance, invade user privacy, and create a disruptive user experience. Users may unwittingly consent to these practices by accepting lengthy end-user license agreements (EULAs) or overlooking installation prompts, highlighting the importance of exercising caution when downloading and installing free software.

Privacy Concerns: Data Collection and Tracking Practices

In the digital age, privacy has become a scarce commodity, particularly concerning free software offerings that may collect and monetize user data. Developers often embed tracking mechanisms or telemetry features within free applications to gather user metrics, usage patterns, and demographic information. While ostensibly aimed at improving user experience or optimizing software performance, these practices raise significant privacy concerns.

Users may unknowingly disclose sensitive information, such as browsing habits, geographic location, or device identifiers, to third parties without adequate transparency or consent mechanisms. Data breaches or unauthorized data sharing incidents involving free software developers have underscored the need for vigilant privacy protection measures. As such, users must scrutinize privacy policies, opt-out of data sharing where possible, and consider the implications of data collection practices before installing free software applications.

Software Reliability and Support: Maintenance and Update Challenges

The reliability and longevity of free software are often contingent upon community support, developer commitment, or corporate sponsorship. Unlike commercial software backed by service-level agreements (SLAs) and dedicated technical support, free applications may lack timely updates, bug fixes, or compatibility enhancements. Developers may discontinue support for older versions or abandon projects altogether, leaving users vulnerable to emerging security threats or compatibility issues with evolving operating systems.

Moreover, the absence of formal support channels or structured maintenance schedules can complicate troubleshooting efforts and prolong resolution times for software-related issues. Users reliant on free software for critical tasks or professional endeavors may face operational disruptions or productivity losses in the absence of adequate technical support mechanisms.

Legal and Licensing Considerations: Compliance and Redistribution Rights

Free software is governed by a diverse array of licensing agreements, ranging from permissive open-source licenses (e.g., MIT, BSD) to copyleft licenses (e.g., GNU General Public License). Understanding the terms of these licenses is crucial, as they dictate permissible uses, redistribution rights, and obligations imposed on both developers and end users.

Failure to comply with licensing terms or inadvertently redistributing software in violation of license agreements can result in legal ramifications, including copyright infringement claims or contractual disputes. Users must exercise diligence when redistributing, modifying, or integrating free software components into proprietary projects to avoid unintended legal consequences.

Mitigating Risks: Best Practices for Safely Using Free Software

Despite the inherent risks, users can mitigate potential threats associated with free software by adopting proactive strategies and best practices:

1. Source Verification and Reputation Assessment: Prioritize downloading free software from reputable sources, official websites, or trusted repositories endorsed by the software's developers or maintainers. Verify the authenticity of downloads to mitigate the risk of downloading counterfeit or tampered software packages.

2. Review Permissions and Privacy Settings:
Before installation, carefully review application permissions and privacy settings to understand the scope of data access requested by the software. Opt-out of data collection features or disable unnecessary permissions that may compromise user privacy.

3. Regular Updates and Security Patches: Maintain up-to-date software installations by applying security patches, updates, or bug fixes released by developers. Enable automatic updates where available to mitigate vulnerabilities and address known security issues promptly.

4. Security Software and Malware Detection:
Deploy reputable antivirus software or anti-malware solutions equipped with real-time scanning capabilities to detect and remove malicious software, adware, or PUPs before they compromise system integrity or user data.

5. User Education and Awareness: Educate users about the risks associated with free software, emphasizing the importance of discernment, skepticism toward unsolicited software offers, and adherence to safe computing practices.

Conclusion

In conclusion, while free software offers compelling benefits and accessibility advantages, users must remain vigilant against inherent risks that threaten security, privacy, and operational continuity.

By understanding the dynamics of free software ecosystems, adhering to best practices for risk mitigation, and maintaining informed decision-making processes, users can navigate the digital landscape responsibly.

The evolving nature of cybersecurity threats necessitates continuous vigilance and adaptation to safeguard personal and organizational interests in an interconnected world shaped by the prevalence of free software offerings.

Chapter 13: Safely Downloading and Installing Software

In today's interconnected digital landscape, downloading and installing software has become an integral part of everyday computing. Whether for personal use, professional tasks, or entertainment purposes, the process of acquiring software demands careful consideration and adherence to best practices to mitigate risks and ensure a seamless user experience. This chapter explores essential strategies and precautions for safely downloading and installing software, emphasizing security, privacy, and operational integrity.

Understanding the Risks: Security and Privacy Implications

Before embarking on the journey of downloading software, it's crucial to understand the inherent risks associated with the process. Malicious actors leverage software distribution channels to disseminate malware, adware, or potentially unwanted programs (PUPs) disguised as legitimate software. These threats can compromise system integrity, steal sensitive information, or render devices vulnerable to exploitation.

Moreover, software installations often require user permissions and access rights, which, if exploited, can grant unauthorized entities control over system resources or compromise user privacy. Privacy concerns extend to data collection practices embedded within software applications, where inadequate transparency or consent mechanisms may result in the unauthorized harvesting of personal information.

Trusted Sources and Software Repositories

A fundamental principle of safe software acquisition is sourcing applications from reputable and trusted sources. Official websites of software developers, recognized app stores, or reputable download repositories maintained by trusted organizations offer a degree of assurance regarding software authenticity and integrity.

When exploring alternative sources, exercise caution and verify the legitimacy of download links to avoid counterfeit or tampered software packages. Avoid downloading software from unverified third-party websites or peer-to-peer (P2P) networks, as these platforms often host compromised or malicious software bundles that pose significant security risks.

Verifying Software Authenticity and Integrity

Before initiating a software download, take proactive measures to verify its authenticity and integrity. Confirm the developer's identity and reputation by reviewing online resources, user reviews, or professional recommendations. Official software repositories typically display digital signatures or checksums—a unique alphanumeric value computed from the software file—to verify the integrity of downloaded files against tampering or corruption during transmission.

Digital signatures attest to the software's authenticity, ensuring it originates from the developer and has not been altered by unauthorized parties. Validate digital signatures using cryptographic tools or built-in verification mechanisms provided by operating systems or security software to mitigate the risk of inadvertently installing malicious software variants.

Understanding Software Installation Processes

Software installation encompasses a series of steps designed to deploy applications on computing devices effectively. During installation, exercise diligence when navigating setup wizards or installation prompts to make informed decisions regarding software configuration, optional features, or bundled components.

Read and comprehend end-user license agreements (EULAs) accompanying software installations to understand licensing terms, usage rights, and obligations imposed on users. Scrutinize permission requests or access requirements specified by the software to prevent inadvertent disclosure of sensitive information or unauthorized system modifications.

Configuring Security and Privacy Settings

Enhance software security and privacy by configuring application settings and permissions according to personal preferences or organizational guidelines. Restrict application permissions to essential functionalities required for intended use cases, minimizing exposure to potential exploits or data breaches. Adjust privacy settings within software applications to limit data collection practices or disable telemetry features that may compromise user privacy without contributing to software functionality or performance.

Implementing Software Updates and Patch Management

Maintain software installations by applying timely updates, security patches, or bug fixes released by developers or software vendors. Enable automatic update mechanisms provided by operating systems or software applications to streamline the deployment of critical updates and mitigate vulnerabilities exposed through security advisories or threat disclosures.

Regularly monitor software update notifications or release notes to identify patches addressing known security vulnerabilities or stability issues affecting installed applications. Prioritize updating software critical to operational workflows or integral to safeguarding sensitive information against emerging threats or evolving attack vectors targeting outdated software versions.

Utilizing Antivirus and Security Software

Fortify device security and safeguard against malicious software threats by deploying reputable antivirus or endpoint protection solutions equipped with real-time scanning capabilities. Configure antivirus software to perform comprehensive system scans, detect suspicious files or behaviors indicative of malware infections, and quarantine or remove identified threats to restore system integrity and prevent further compromise.

Schedule regular virus definition updates or database refreshes to ensure antivirus software maintains current threat intelligence and effectively identifies new or evolving malware variants. Leverage additional security features, such as web protection modules or email scanning functionalities, integrated within antivirus solutions to proactively mitigate risks associated with online threats, phishing attacks, or malicious software downloads.

Educating Users and Promoting Security Awareness

Foster a culture of cybersecurity awareness and informed decision-making among users to promote safe practices when downloading and installing software. Educate users on identifying red flags indicative of potentially malicious software, such as unsolicited download prompts, misleading advertisements, or suspicious file extensions commonly associated with malware distribution.

Encourage users to seek guidance from IT support personnel or cybersecurity professionals when uncertain about software authenticity, installation procedures, or security implications. Provide training sessions, informative resources, or interactive workshops addressing common cybersecurity threats, best practices for software hygiene, and proactive measures to mitigate risks encountered during software acquisition or deployment.

Conclusion

In conclusion, safely downloading and installing software hinges on proactive risk management, informed decision-making, and adherence to established best practices designed to safeguard system integrity, protect user privacy, and mitigate cybersecurity threats.

By sourcing software from trusted sources, verifying authenticity through digital signatures, and exercising diligence during installation and configuration processes, users can fortify defenses against malicious software threats and ensure the continued reliability of software applications critical to personal or organizational operations.

Embrace the evolving landscape of cybersecurity awareness and educational initiatives to empower users with the knowledge and skills necessary to navigate digital environments responsibly and contribute to a secure computing ecosystem.

Chapter 14: Handling Email Attachments Safely

Email attachments serve as convenient tools for sharing documents, images, and files across digital platforms. However, they also pose significant cybersecurity risks, ranging from malware infections to phishing attacks designed to compromise sensitive information or infiltrate computing systems. This chapter explores essential strategies and best practices for safely handling email attachments, emphasizing proactive measures to mitigate risks, ensure data integrity, and protect against evolving cyber threats.

Understanding Email Attachments: Types and Risks

Email attachments encompass a broad spectrum of file types, including documents (e.g., PDFs, Word files), spreadsheets, images, compressed archives (e.g., ZIP files), and executable programs (e.g., .exe files). While attachments facilitate seamless information exchange and collaboration, they introduce inherent security vulnerabilities exploited by malicious actors seeking to exploit unsuspecting users.

Common risks associated with email attachments include:

1. Malware Distribution: Malicious attachments may contain viruses, worms, ransomware, or trojans designed to compromise system integrity, steal sensitive data, or disrupt operations. Malware payloads embedded within attachments exploit software vulnerabilities or user actions (e.g., clicking links, executing files) to infiltrate devices and propagate across networks.

2. Phishing and Social Engineering: Email attachments serve as vehicles for phishing campaigns employing deceptive tactics to lure recipients into divulging confidential information or initiating unauthorized actions.

Phishing attachments masquerade as legitimate files (e.g., invoices, shipping notifications) to deceive users into opening malicious content or disclosing login credentials, financial details, or personal data.

3. File-Based Attacks: File-based attacks leverage vulnerabilities inherent in specific file formats (e.g., macros in Office documents) to execute malicious scripts, initiate unauthorized downloads, or exploit software weaknesses.

Attackers manipulate file attributes or content to evade detection by antivirus software and leverage trusted communication channels (e.g., email) to disseminate malicious payloads.

Best Practices for Handling Email Attachments

Implementing proactive strategies and adopting best practices enhances email attachment security, mitigates associated risks, and safeguards organizational or personal data against cyber threats:

1. Verify Sender Identity and Email Authenticity: Exercise caution when receiving unsolicited emails or attachments from unknown or unexpected senders. Verify sender identities and email authenticity by scrutinizing email addresses, domain names, or sender information displayed in email headers. Beware of spoofed or forged email addresses mimicking trusted entities to deceive recipients into opening malicious attachments.

2. Exercise Skepticism Toward Unsolicited Attachments: Exercise skepticism toward unsolicited attachments or unexpected file attachments received from unfamiliar sources, even if seemingly legitimate or contextually relevant. Verify the necessity and legitimacy of attachments with senders through alternative communication channels (e.g., phone calls, official websites) before opening or accessing potentially malicious content.

3. Scan Email Attachments for Malware: Leverage antivirus software or endpoint protection solutions equipped with email scanning capabilities to detect and mitigate malware threats embedded within email attachments. Configure antivirus settings to perform real-time scanning of incoming email attachments, quarantine suspicious files, and promptly alert users or administrators of potential security risks.

4. Disable Automatic Execution of File Downloads: Configure email client settings or security preferences to disable automatic execution of file downloads or attachments upon receipt. Implement default settings requiring user consent or manual interaction to initiate file downloads, open attachments, or execute embedded scripts to mitigate inadvertent exposure to malware or file-based attacks.

5. Educate Users on Safe Attachment Handling Practices: Promote cybersecurity awareness and educate users on safe attachment handling practices to foster a culture of vigilance and informed decision-making. Provide training sessions, informational resources, or interactive workshops addressing common email attachment risks, phishing indicators, and preventive measures to mitigate threats encountered in daily communication routines.

6. Implement File Type Restrictions and Filtering Policies: Implement email security policies or filtering mechanisms to restrict or filter attachment file types based on organizational requirements, risk assessments, or regulatory compliance mandates. Configure email gateways, spam filters, or content filtering solutions to block potentially malicious file extensions (e.g., .exe, .js) or file types prone to exploitation (e.g., macro-enabled Office documents) from entering organizational networks or endpoints.

7. Regularly Update Software and Security Patches: Maintain up-to-date software installations, security patches, or firmware updates for email clients, antivirus solutions, operating systems, and network infrastructure to mitigate vulnerabilities exploited by email attachment-based attacks. Enable automatic updates or patch management mechanisms to ensure timely deployment of critical security updates addressing known vulnerabilities or emerging threats impacting email attachment security.

Incident Response and Remediation Strategies

Despite proactive measures, incidents involving malicious email attachments may occur, necessitating swift incident response and remediation strategies to minimize impact and restore operational continuity:

1. Incident Identification and Triage: Promptly identify and triage suspected email attachment-related incidents through real-time monitoring, security alerts, or user-reported indicators of compromise (IOCs). Collaborate with incident response teams, IT security personnel, or cybersecurity experts to assess incident severity, ascertain attack vectors, and initiate response protocols.

2. Quarantine and Containment Measures: Isolate or quarantine affected email attachments, devices, or network segments to prevent lateral movement, mitigate propagation of malware infections, and preserve digital evidence for forensic analysis or incident investigation purposes. Implement containment measures to limit impact, disrupt attack vectors, and restore secure operational environments while mitigating potential data loss or compromise.

3. Incident Mitigation and Recovery Actions: Execute incident mitigation and recovery actions tailored to identified threat vectors, attack methodologies, or compromised assets impacted by malicious email attachments. Implement remediation strategies, restore system integrity, and validate effectiveness of security controls or countermeasures deployed to prevent recurrence of similar incidents in the future.

4. Post-Incident Analysis and Lessons Learned:
Conduct post-incident analysis, root cause analysis (RCA), or lessons learned sessions to evaluate incident response effectiveness, identify procedural improvements, and enhance organizational resilience against email attachment-related threats. Document findings, recommendations, or corrective actions to refine incident response plans, strengthen cybersecurity posture, and reinforce user awareness of email attachment security best practices.

Conclusion

In conclusion, safely handling email attachments requires vigilance, informed decision-making, and proactive adoption of cybersecurity best practices to mitigate risks, safeguard sensitive information, and protect against evolving cyber threats.

By verifying sender authenticity, scanning attachments for malware, disabling automatic execution of downloads, and educating users on safe attachment handling practices, individuals and organizations can fortify defenses, promote cybersecurity awareness, and maintain secure communication environments essential to operational resilience and digital well-being.

Embrace a proactive approach to email attachment security, integrate incident response capabilities, and continuously evolve strategies to mitigate emerging threats in an interconnected digital landscape shaped by the prevalence of email communication and information exchange.

Chapter 15: The Danger of Malicious Links in Emails and Messages

In the digital age, where communication thrives across diverse platforms, the ubiquitous presence of malicious links in emails and messages poses a pervasive threat to cybersecurity. These deceptive links, concealed within seemingly innocuous communications, exploit human curiosity, trust, and complacency to infiltrate systems, compromise sensitive information, and propagate malicious activities. This chapter explores the multifaceted dangers associated with malicious links, delves into common attack methodologies employed by threat actors, and delineates proactive strategies for identifying, mitigating, and mitigating these pervasive cyber threats.

Understanding Malicious Links: Methods and Objectives

Malicious links embedded in emails and messages serve as conduits for cyber threats, leveraging social engineering tactics and deceptive techniques to exploit user vulnerabilities. Threat actors manipulate human psychology, urgency, or curiosity to entice recipients into clicking on malicious links, thereby facilitating unauthorized access, data exfiltration, or installation of malware onto devices and networks.

Common objectives of malicious link attacks include:

1. Phishing Attacks: Phishing campaigns leverage deceptive links disguised as legitimate websites or trusted entities to deceive users into disclosing confidential information, such as login credentials, financial details, or personal data. Phishing links mimic familiar interfaces (e.g., banking portals, social media platforms) to elicit user trust and bypass vigilance, facilitating identity theft or financial fraud schemes.

2. Malware Distribution: Malicious links may initiate malware downloads, execute malicious scripts, or exploit software vulnerabilities to compromise system integrity, steal sensitive data, or establish unauthorized access. Malware payloads distributed via malicious links encompass ransomware, trojans, spyware, or botnets designed to exploit user actions (e.g., clicking links, downloading files) and propagate across networks.

3. Credential Harvesting: Links embedded in phishing emails or deceptive messages may redirect users to counterfeit login pages or credential harvesting sites designed to capture user credentials upon submission. Threat actors harvest stolen credentials to perpetrate account takeovers, unauthorized access, or subsequent phishing attacks targeting contacts within compromised networks.

Attack Vectors and Methodologies

Malicious links exploit diverse attack vectors and methodologies to evade detection, circumvent security controls, and exploit human vulnerabilities inherent in digital communication channels:

1. Email Spoofing and Impersonation: Threat actors employ email spoofing techniques to forge sender identities or mimic trusted entities, deceiving recipients into believing deceptive links originate from legitimate sources. Impersonation tactics leverage familiarity or authority associated with trusted brands, colleagues, or service providers to lower recipient defenses and increase likelihood of link engagement.

2. URL Obfuscation and Redirection: Malicious links obfuscate URLs using URL shortening services, encoded characters, or redirection techniques to conceal true destinations and evade detection by security filters or email scanners. URL redirection chains or domain hopping tactics redirect users through multiple intermediary sites before landing on malicious landing pages hosting exploit kits, phishing forms, or malware payloads.

3. Social Engineering Tactics: Social engineering tactics exploit emotional triggers, urgency, or curiosity to manipulate user behavior and elicit unwarranted clicks on malicious links. Threat actors craft persuasive narratives (e.g., urgent notifications, enticing offers) within emails or messages to evoke fear, excitement, or curiosity, compelling recipients to bypass cautionary instincts and engage with malicious content.

Identifying and Mitigating Malicious Links

Effective mitigation of malicious link threats necessitates proactive identification, vigilant scrutiny, and adherence to cybersecurity best practices designed to safeguard personal or organizational interests:

1. Verify Sender Authenticity and Email Context: Verify sender authenticity by scrutinizing email addresses, domain names, or sender information displayed in email headers for discrepancies or inconsistencies indicative of spoofed identities. Exercise caution toward unsolicited emails, unexpected attachments, or messages containing vague or urgent requests prompting link engagement.

2. Hover Over Links for URL Inspection: Hover over embedded links within emails or messages to reveal underlying URLs and evaluate destination legitimacy before clicking. Inspect URLs for irregularities (e.g., misspellings, alphanumeric strings) or deceptive practices employed to mask true destinations, redirect users, or initiate malicious activities upon click-through.

3. Exercise Skepticism Toward Unsolicited Links: Exercise skepticism toward unsolicited links or unexpected messages received from unfamiliar or unverified sources, even if seemingly relevant or contextually plausible. Refrain from clicking on links embedded within unsolicited emails, social media messages, or instant messaging platforms lacking sufficient sender validation or identifiable context.

4. Implement URL Filtering and Web Security Controls: Deploy URL filtering solutions, web security gateways, or endpoint protection tools equipped with malicious link detection capabilities to intercept and block access to known malicious URLs or phishing domains. Configure security controls to enforce URL categorization policies, restrict access to high-risk websites, and mitigate exposure to malicious link-based threats across organizational networks or endpoints.

5. Educate Users on Link Awareness and Cybersecurity Hygiene: Promote cybersecurity awareness initiatives, user training programs, or interactive workshops emphasizing the dangers of malicious links and best practices for safe link handling. Educate users on identifying phishing indicators, recognizing social engineering tactics, and adopting cautious behaviors to mitigate risks associated with malicious link engagement in digital communications.

Incident Response and Remediation Strategies

In the event of malicious link engagement or suspected compromise, implement incident response strategies to mitigate impact, preserve digital evidence, and restore operational integrity:

1. Disconnect from Network Access: Immediately disconnect compromised devices from network access to prevent further propagation of malware, data exfiltration, or unauthorized access within organizational environments. Isolate affected systems to contain incident impact and mitigate potential cross-contamination across interconnected networks or shared resources.

2. Perform System Scans and Malware Remediation: Initiate comprehensive system scans using antivirus software, endpoint protection tools, or malware detection utilities to identify and remove malicious software infections resulting from link engagement. Quarantine suspicious files, remediate compromised system configurations, and restore affected devices to secure operational states following malware removal procedures.

3. Incident Analysis and Threat Intelligence Gathering: Conduct post-incident analysis, forensic examinations, or threat intelligence gathering to ascertain attack vectors, determine breach extent, and identify vulnerabilities exploited during malicious link engagement. Document incident findings, prioritize remediation efforts, and leverage threat intelligence insights to fortify defenses against future malicious link-based threats.

Conclusion

In conclusion, the pervasive threat posed by malicious links in emails and messages underscores the critical importance of vigilance, education, and proactive cybersecurity measures in safeguarding digital environments against evolving cyber threats.

By understanding attack methodologies, identifying phishing indicators, and implementing robust mitigation strategies, individuals and organizations can mitigate risks associated with malicious link engagement, preserve data integrity, and fortify defenses against social engineering tactics exploiting human vulnerabilities in digital communication channels.

Embrace a proactive approach to link awareness, foster cybersecurity resilience, and empower users with the knowledge and tools necessary to navigate digital landscapes safely while preserving confidentiality, integrity, and availability of sensitive information in an interconnected world shaped by ubiquitous communication technologies.

Chapter 16: Recognizing and Avoiding Malvertising

In the digital age, where browsing the internet is an integral part of daily life, the threat of malvertising lurks behind seemingly innocent clicks. Malvertising, a portmanteau of "malicious advertising," refers to online advertisements that contain malicious code designed to infect computers or steal personal information. This chapter explores what malvertising is, how to recognize it, and practical strategies to avoid falling victim to its traps.

Understanding Malvertising

Malvertising operates surreptitiously, exploiting the trust users place in online ads displayed on legitimate websites. These malicious ads can take various forms, from banner ads to pop-ups and auto-redirects. Cybercriminals use malvertising to distribute malware such as ransomware, spyware, or adware, targeting vulnerabilities in web browsers and plugins. Unlike traditional malware distribution methods, malvertising leverages the vast reach of online advertising networks to reach millions of potential victims.

Signs of Malvertising

Recognizing malvertising requires vigilance and an understanding of its common characteristics. One telltale sign is ads that redirect unexpectedly to unfamiliar websites, especially if these sites prompt downloads or request sensitive information. Another indicator is ads that mimic system alerts or error messages, urging users to take immediate action, such as clicking on a link or downloading a file. Additionally, unusually high CPU usage or browser crashes after encountering specific ads may indicate malicious activity.

Vulnerable Platforms and Attack Vectors

While malvertising can affect any internet user, certain platforms and browsing habits increase the risk. For instance, older versions of web browsers or plugins often have unpatched security vulnerabilities that malvertisers exploit. Similarly, visiting less secure websites or clicking on ads from dubious sources amplifies the likelihood of exposure to malicious content. Mobile devices, with their smaller screens and often less stringent security measures, are also prime targets for malvertising campaigns.

Mitigating Risks: Best Practices

Protecting against malvertising begins with adopting proactive cybersecurity practices. Keeping software, including web browsers, plugins, and operating systems, updated with the latest security patches is crucial. Installing reputable ad blockers can significantly reduce exposure to malicious ads, although users should be mindful of their chosen ad blocker's credibility to avoid inadvertently installing malware disguised as protective software.

Browser and Device Security

Configuring browsers and devices with robust security settings adds an additional layer of defense against malvertising. Enabling browser security features such as pop-up blockers and sandboxed browsing environments limits the execution of potentially harmful scripts and codes. Moreover, configuring devices to restrict automatic downloads and prompt for user consent before executing scripts or accessing certain types of content enhances control over online interactions, mitigating the risk of unintended exposure to malvertising.

Adherence to Safe Browsing Practices

Practicing safe browsing habits is essential for minimizing exposure to malvertising. Avoid clicking on ads from unfamiliar or untrusted sources, especially those promising unrealistic offers or incentives.

Exercise caution when visiting websites that frequently display intrusive or misleading ads, as these platforms may prioritize ad revenue over user security. Furthermore, scrutinizing URL domains and ensuring they match the expected content can help identify potentially malicious redirects or phishing attempts disguised as legitimate advertising.

Educating End Users

Educating end users about the risks associated with malvertising fosters a culture of cybersecurity awareness. Encouraging individuals to remain vigilant while browsing online, particularly when interacting with advertisements, empowers them to recognize suspicious behaviors and take appropriate action.

Teaching users to verify the legitimacy of ads and promptly report suspicious activities to website administrators or cybersecurity experts contributes to collective efforts in combating malvertising and protecting online communities.

Collaborative Efforts in Cybersecurity

Addressing the pervasive threat of malvertising requires collaborative efforts among internet service providers (ISPs), advertising networks, cybersecurity firms, and regulatory authorities. Implementing industry-wide standards for ad verification and deploying advanced detection technologies, such as machine learning algorithms capable of identifying anomalous ad behaviors, strengthens defenses against evolving malvertising tactics.

Additionally, fostering transparency in ad networks regarding the sources and content of displayed ads promotes accountability and builds trust among users.

Conclusion

In conclusion, recognizing and avoiding malvertising demands a proactive approach to cybersecurity that encompasses awareness, education, and adherence to best practices.

By understanding the nature of malvertising, identifying its warning signs, and implementing effective mitigation strategies, individuals and organizations can safeguard against potential threats posed by malicious online advertisements. Through continuous vigilance and collaboration across sectors, we can collectively mitigate the impact of malvertising and foster a safer digital ecosystem for all users.

Chapter 17: Keeping Your Operating System Secure

In the interconnected world of today, where digital landscapes are ubiquitous and essential, securing your operating system (OS) is paramount to safeguarding personal and professional data from malicious threats. This chapter explores essential strategies and practices to keep your OS secure, ensuring resilience against cyber threats and maintaining the integrity of your digital footprint.

Understanding Operating System Security

Operating system security refers to the measures and configurations designed to protect the OS against unauthorized access, malicious attacks, and data breaches. Whether you use Windows, macOS, Linux, or another OS, each requires diligent management and adherence to security best practices to mitigate vulnerabilities and defend against evolving cyber threats.

Importance of Regular Updates and Patching

One of the foundational pillars of OS security is keeping it up-to-date with the latest patches and security updates. Software developers frequently release updates to address newly discovered vulnerabilities and weaknesses that cybercriminals exploit. By promptly installing updates from trusted sources, users ensure that their OS remains fortified against known threats and exploits, reducing the risk of unauthorized access or data compromise.

Strengthening User Authentication and Access Controls

Effective user authentication mechanisms are essential to prevent unauthorized access to sensitive data and system resources. Implementing strong passwords or passphrase policies, including multi-factor authentication (MFA) where possible, enhances user verification beyond mere password strength. Additionally, limiting user privileges to only those necessary for their roles and responsibilities minimizes the impact of potential security breaches and unauthorized activities within the OS environment.

Configuring Firewall and Network Security Settings

OS security encompasses safeguarding network connectivity and communications through robust firewall configurations and network security settings. Firewalls act as gatekeepers, monitoring and filtering incoming and outgoing network traffic based on predefined security rules. Configuring firewalls to block unauthorized access attempts and suspicious connections helps thwart malicious activities, such as unauthorized data exfiltration or remote exploitation of system vulnerabilities.

Implementing Antivirus and Anti-malware Solutions

Deploying reputable antivirus and anti-malware software remains crucial in detecting and neutralizing malicious software threats targeting the OS. These security solutions scan files, programs, and system processes for signs of malware, including viruses, worms, Trojans, and ransomware. Regularly updating antivirus definitions and performing scheduled scans enhance the software's efficacy in identifying and mitigating emerging malware strains, thereby fortifying OS defenses against potential cyber attacks.

Data Encryption and Backup Strategies

Protecting sensitive data stored on the OS requires implementing robust encryption protocols to render information unreadable to unauthorized entities. Encryption algorithms encrypt data at rest and in transit, safeguarding confidential files and communications from interception or unauthorized access. Additionally, establishing routine data backup procedures ensures the availability and integrity of critical information in the event of hardware failures, ransomware attacks, or data breaches, enabling prompt restoration and continuity of operations.

Monitoring System Logs and Security Events

Monitoring system logs and security events provides valuable insights into OS activities, user interactions, and potential security incidents. OS logging mechanisms record events such as login attempts, file modifications, and network connections, facilitating proactive detection of suspicious behaviors or anomalies indicative of unauthorized access or compromise. Analyzing logged data and security event notifications enables timely incident response and remediation actions to mitigate the impact of security breaches and prevent future occurrences.

Educating and Promoting Cybersecurity Awareness

Promoting cybersecurity awareness among users is instrumental in cultivating a security-conscious culture and minimizing human error vulnerabilities. Educating individuals on recognizing phishing attempts, practicing safe browsing habits, and adhering to organizational security policies enhances their ability to identify and mitigate potential OS security risks proactively. Encouraging users to report suspicious activities promptly and participate in ongoing cybersecurity training initiatives fosters a collaborative approach to maintaining OS security and resilience against evolving cyber threats.

Implementing System Hardening and Vulnerability Management

System hardening involves configuring the OS environment to minimize attack surfaces and strengthen security posture against potential exploits. This includes disabling unnecessary services, removing or disabling default accounts and passwords, and applying security configuration baselines recommended by OS vendors or cybersecurity frameworks. Conducting regular vulnerability assessments and penetration testing helps identify and address OS vulnerabilities before they can be exploited maliciously, reinforcing proactive defense strategies and ensuring continuous OS security improvement.

Collaborative Efforts in OS Security

Effective OS security requires collaboration among OS developers, cybersecurity experts, regulatory bodies, and end users to address emerging threats and implement resilient security measures. Participating in OS vendor security programs, sharing threat intelligence within cybersecurity communities, and adhering to industry standards and regulatory guidelines contribute to collective efforts in safeguarding OS environments from sophisticated cyber attacks and ensuring the trustworthiness of digital interactions and transactions.

Conclusion

In conclusion, safeguarding your operating system against cyber threats demands a multifaceted approach encompassing proactive security measures, continuous vigilance, and user education.

By understanding the importance of OS security, implementing robust security controls and best practices, and fostering a culture of cybersecurity awareness, individuals and organizations can mitigate risks, protect sensitive information, and uphold the integrity of their digital environments.

Through concerted efforts and collaboration across sectors, we can collectively strengthen OS security frameworks, adapt to evolving cyber threats, and cultivate a safer digital landscape for all users.

Chapter 18: Using Secure Wi-Fi Networks

In the modern era of ubiquitous connectivity, Wi-Fi networks have become essential for accessing the internet and conducting various online activities. However, the convenience of wireless connectivity comes with inherent security risks. This chapter delves into the importance of using secure Wi-Fi networks, outlines potential threats associated with unsecured connections, and offers practical strategies to enhance Wi-Fi security.

Understanding Wi-Fi Security Risks

Wi-Fi networks transmit data wirelessly, making them susceptible to interception by unauthorized individuals or malicious entities. Unsecured Wi-Fi connections, such as those without encryption or weak authentication mechanisms, pose significant risks to users' privacy and data integrity. Cybercriminals exploit vulnerabilities in unsecured Wi-Fi networks to eavesdrop on communications, steal sensitive information (e.g., passwords, financial data), or launch sophisticated cyber attacks, including man-in-the-middle (MITM) attacks and session hijacking.

Importance of Wi-Fi Encryption Protocols

Implementing robust encryption protocols is fundamental to securing Wi-Fi communications and protecting data transmitted over wireless networks. Wi-Fi Protected Access (WPA) and WPA2 are widely adopted encryption standards that encrypt data between devices and wireless access points, mitigating the risk of unauthorized interception or tampering. Employing strong encryption methods, such as AES (Advanced Encryption Standard), ensures confidentiality and integrity of transmitted data, safeguarding against malicious interception and exploitation of network vulnerabilities.

Securing Wi-Fi Access Points

Securing Wi-Fi access points (APs) is critical in preventing unauthorized access and maintaining network integrity. Changing default administrative credentials and using complex passwords or passphrases for Wi-Fi access point configurations mitigate the risk of unauthorized configuration changes or malicious access. Disabling Wi-Fi Protected Setup (WPS) and configuring access points to use enterprise-grade security protocols, such as IEEE 802.1X authentication, further strengthens access control mechanisms and enhances network security against unauthorized intrusions.

Configuring Wireless Network Encryption

Configuring Wi-Fi networks with strong encryption settings is essential for safeguarding data confidentiality and preventing unauthorized access. Choosing WPA3 encryption, the latest Wi-Fi security standard, enhances protection against brute-force attacks and improves resilience against cryptographic vulnerabilities. Enabling encryption protocols such as WPA3-Personal or WPA3-Enterprise and using long, complex pre-shared keys (PSKs) or implementing certificate-based authentication for enterprise environments fortify Wi-Fi security measures and mitigate risks associated with unsecured wireless communications.

Implementing Network Segmentation and Isolation

Segmenting Wi-Fi networks into distinct virtual LANs (VLANs) or subnets isolates sensitive devices and restricts unauthorized access to critical network resources. Implementing network segmentation strategies separates guest Wi-Fi networks from internal corporate networks, limiting potential exposure to unauthorized users and reducing the impact of security breaches. Configuring firewall rules and access control lists (ACLs) to restrict inter-VLAN communication and enforce network segmentation policies enhances network security posture and mitigates risks associated with unauthorized access or lateral movement within segmented network environments.

Monitoring Wi-Fi Network Traffic and Activity

Monitoring Wi-Fi network traffic and activity provides real-time visibility into network operations and detects anomalous behaviors indicative of unauthorized access or malicious activities. Deploying intrusion detection systems (IDS) or intrusion prevention systems (IPS) enables continuous monitoring of network traffic patterns and alerts administrators to potential security incidents, such as unauthorized access attempts or network intrusions. Analyzing Wi-Fi network logs and security event notifications facilitates proactive threat detection, incident response, and mitigation of security vulnerabilities or compromised network devices.

Educating Users on Wi-Fi Security Best Practices

Promoting awareness of Wi-Fi security best practices among users is instrumental in fostering a security-conscious culture and mitigating risks associated with unsecured wireless communications. Educating users on recognizing secure Wi-Fi networks, avoiding public Wi-Fi hotspots for transmitting sensitive information, and verifying network encryption protocols before connecting to unfamiliar Wi-Fi networks enhances their ability to make informed decisions and protect personal or organizational data from potential cyber threats. Encouraging users to enable firewall settings, install reputable antivirus software, and apply software updates regularly strengthens their overall cybersecurity posture and reduces susceptibility to Wi-Fi-related security vulnerabilities.

Performing Regular Wi-Fi Security Audits and Assessments

Conducting regular Wi-Fi security audits and assessments evaluates the effectiveness of implemented security controls and identifies potential vulnerabilities or weaknesses within wireless network infrastructures.

Performing comprehensive vulnerability scans, penetration testing, or wireless site surveys assesses network security posture, identifies unauthorized access points or rogue devices, and verifies compliance with established security policies and regulatory requirements.

Implementing remediation actions based on audit findings strengthens Wi-Fi security measures, enhances network resilience against evolving cyber threats, and ensures continuous improvement of wireless network security posture.

Collaborative Efforts in Wi-Fi Security

Enhancing Wi-Fi security requires collaborative efforts among stakeholders, including network administrators, IT security teams, Wi-Fi equipment vendors, and regulatory authorities.

Participating in industry forums, sharing threat intelligence, and adhering to established security standards and best practices promote collective efforts to address emerging Wi-Fi security challenges, mitigate risks associated with wireless communications, and strengthen overall cybersecurity defenses.

Collaborating with Wi-Fi technology providers to implement secure-by-design principles and deploy advanced encryption protocols fosters innovation in Wi-Fi security solutions and ensures the integrity, confidentiality, and availability of wireless network communications in diverse operational environments.

Conclusion

In conclusion, using secure Wi-Fi networks is essential for protecting sensitive data, maintaining privacy, and mitigating risks associated with wireless communications in today's interconnected world.

By understanding the importance of Wi-Fi security, implementing robust encryption protocols, securing Wi-Fi access points, and educating users on best practices, individuals and organizations can enhance their resilience against evolving cyber threats and safeguard against unauthorized access or malicious activities targeting wireless network infrastructures.

Through proactive measures, continuous monitoring, and collaborative efforts across sectors, we can collectively strengthen Wi-Fi security frameworks, promote secure digital interactions, and foster a safer and more resilient wireless network environment for all users.

Chapter 19: The Importance of Regular Backups

In the realm of digital data and information management, the importance of regular backups cannot be overstated. Whether for personal files, business data, or critical system configurations, backups serve as a fundamental safeguard against data loss, system failures, cyber attacks, and unforeseen disasters. This chapter explores the significance of regular backups, the risks associated with inadequate data protection measures, best practices for implementing backup strategies, and the role of backups in ensuring data resilience and business continuity.

Mitigating Risks of Data Loss and Corruption

Data loss can occur due to various factors, including hardware failures, software glitches, accidental deletions, and malicious activities such as ransomware attacks or cyber theft. Without adequate backups, organizations and individuals risk losing valuable information critical to daily operations, financial transactions, intellectual property, and personal memories. Regular backups mitigate the impact of data loss by providing redundant copies of essential data and enabling swift recovery in the event of unforeseen incidents or system failures.

Protecting Against Ransomware and Cyber Threats

In today's digital landscape, ransomware attacks pose a significant threat to data integrity and operational continuity. Ransomware encrypts files or locks access to computer systems, demanding ransom payments in exchange for decryption keys or restored access. Regular backups offer a defense mechanism against ransomware attacks by allowing users to restore encrypted or compromised data from unaffected backup copies. Implementing backup routines that include offline or cloud-based storage solutions enhances data protection and reduces the likelihood of ransomware incidents crippling organizational operations.

Supporting Business Continuity and Disaster Recovery

For businesses and enterprises, maintaining uninterrupted operations and ensuring continuity in service delivery are paramount. Regular backups form the cornerstone of disaster recovery and business continuity planning by preserving critical data and infrastructure configurations necessary for resuming normal business operations following disruptive events. Establishing comprehensive backup and recovery strategies, including offsite backups and replication mechanisms, minimizes downtime, mitigates financial losses, and enhances organizational resilience against unforeseen disasters or operational disruptions.

Compliance with Regulatory Requirements and Data Protection Standards

In an era marked by stringent regulatory frameworks and data protection standards, organizations must comply with legal mandates governing data retention, privacy, and security. Regular backups play a crucial role in meeting compliance requirements by ensuring the availability and integrity of archived data for audit purposes, legal investigations, or regulatory inspections. Implementing backup policies that align with industry-specific regulations, such as GDPR (General Data Protection Regulation) or HIPAA (Health Insurance Portability and Accountability Act), demonstrates organizational commitment to safeguarding sensitive information and mitigating legal liabilities associated with data breaches or non-compliance penalties.

Safeguarding Personal and Professional Assets

Beyond organizational data, individuals also benefit from regular backups to safeguard personal files, digital assets, and sentimental memories stored on electronic devices. Photos, videos, documents, and personal records accumulated over time hold significant sentimental and practical value. Implementing automated backup solutions or cloud-based storage services ensures the preservation of cherished memories and important documents against device failures, accidental deletions, or loss due to theft or physical damage.

Reducing Recovery Time Objectives (RTO) and Downtime Costs

In business environments, downtime resulting from data loss incidents or system outages can incur substantial financial costs and operational disruptions. Regular backups reduce Recovery Time Objectives (RTO) by facilitating expedited data recovery and minimizing the duration of service interruptions. Leveraging backup technologies, such as incremental or differential backups, accelerates data restoration processes and enables organizations to resume critical operations swiftly, thereby mitigating revenue losses, preserving customer trust, and maintaining competitive edge in dynamic market landscapes.

Implementing Robust Backup Strategies and Best Practices

Effective backup strategies encompass a combination of technological solutions, procedural protocols, and organizational policies tailored to meet specific data protection objectives and operational requirements. Designing backup schedules that prioritize frequent data backups, including real-time or continuous data protection mechanisms, enhances data availability and minimizes data loss exposures. Employing encryption protocols and access controls for stored backup data safeguards against unauthorized access or data breaches, reinforcing overall data security posture and compliance with privacy regulations.

Leveraging Cloud-Based Backup Services and Storage Solutions

Cloud-based backup services offer scalable and cost-effective solutions for storing and managing backup data across geographically dispersed locations.

Leveraging cloud storage solutions provides inherent advantages, such as automated data replication, remote accessibility, and disaster recovery capabilities, without the overhead costs associated with maintaining on-premises backup infrastructure. Integrating hybrid backup architectures that combine cloud-based and local storage repositories ensures redundancy, enhances data resilience, and facilitates seamless data recovery operations in diverse operational environments.

Educating Users on Backup Best Practices and Data Hygiene

Promoting user awareness and adherence to backup best practices are integral to cultivating a proactive data protection culture within organizations and among individuals.

Educating users on the importance of regular backups, data hygiene practices, and disaster preparedness measures empowers them to actively participate in safeguarding data integrity and mitigating risks of data loss incidents. Conducting periodic training sessions, disseminating backup guidelines, and implementing data recovery drills foster a collaborative approach to data resilience and enhance organizational readiness to respond effectively to evolving cyber threats or operational disruptions.

Conclusion

In conclusion, regular backups are indispensable for protecting data assets, ensuring operational continuity, and mitigating risks associated with data loss incidents, cyber attacks, and unforeseen disasters.

By implementing robust backup strategies, leveraging advanced backup technologies, and fostering a culture of data protection awareness, organizations and individuals can safeguard critical information, preserve business continuity, and uphold regulatory compliance obligations.

Embracing proactive data protection measures and investing in resilient backup solutions empower stakeholders to navigate digital challenges confidently and sustainably in an increasingly interconnected and data-driven world.

Chapter 20: Securing Your Mobile Devices Against Malware

Mobile devices have become indispensable tools in daily life, serving as portals to vast amounts of personal and professional information. However, their widespread use and connectivity make them prime targets for malware and cyber attacks. This chapter explores essential strategies for securing mobile devices against malware, the types of threats encountered in the mobile ecosystem, best practices for prevention and mitigation, and the role of user education in maintaining mobile device security.

Understanding Mobile Malware Threats

Mobile malware encompasses malicious software specifically designed to exploit vulnerabilities in mobile operating systems (OS) and applications. Common types of mobile malware include viruses, Trojans, ransomware, adware, and spyware, each posing unique risks to device security and user privacy. Mobile malware infections can compromise sensitive data, track user activities, hijack device functions, or facilitate unauthorized access to personal information, emphasizing the importance of proactive mobile security measures.

Securing Mobile Operating Systems and Applications

Securing mobile devices begins with maintaining up-to-date operating systems (OS) and applications. Regularly updating mobile OS versions and installing security patches issued by device manufacturers or OS developers mitigates vulnerabilities exploited by malware authors. Configuring automatic updates ensures timely deployment of critical security fixes and enhances device resilience against emerging threats or exploit techniques targeting outdated software components.

Installing Reputable Antivirus and Mobile Security Software

Deploying reputable antivirus and mobile security software enhances proactive defense mechanisms against mobile malware threats. Mobile security solutions offer real-time malware scanning, malicious app detection, and web browsing protection features that safeguard against potentially harmful content or suspicious activities. Choosing security applications from trusted vendors with positive industry reviews and implementing supplementary security features, such as anti-theft functionalities or privacy protection tools, reinforces mobile device security posture and reduces susceptibility to malware infections.

Implementing Appropriate App Permissions and Access Controls

Managing app permissions and access controls on mobile devices minimizes the risk of unauthorized data access or exploitation by malicious applications. Reviewing and adjusting app permissions during installation or post-installation ensures apps only access necessary device resources or personal information essential for their intended functionalities. Restricting background app activities, disabling unnecessary app permissions, and periodically auditing installed applications for suspicious behaviors mitigate potential risks associated with excessive app privileges or inadvertent data leakage.

Avoiding Unauthorized App Installations and Third-Party Stores

Limiting app installations to official app stores, such as Google Play Store or Apple App Store, reduces exposure to counterfeit or malicious applications distributed through unauthorized third-party stores. Official app stores implement stringent vetting processes and security measures to verify app authenticity, detect malware-infected apps, and protect users from potential security threats. Sideloading apps from unknown sources or untrusted repositories increases the likelihood of inadvertently installing malware-infected applications capable of compromising device security and compromising user privacy.

Practicing Safe Browsing Habits and Avoiding Phishing Attempts

Practicing safe browsing habits on mobile devices mitigates risks associated with malicious websites, phishing attempts, and fraudulent online activities. Avoiding clicking on suspicious links or advertisements, verifying website authenticity before entering sensitive information, and refraining from downloading files from unknown sources enhance protection against phishing scams, credential theft, or malware distribution campaigns targeting mobile device users. Implementing web browser security settings, such as pop-up blockers or safe browsing modes, reinforces defenses against malicious web content and potential cyber threats.

Enabling Device Encryption and Secure Authentication Mechanisms

Enabling device encryption and implementing secure authentication mechanisms strengthen mobile device security posture against unauthorized access attempts or data breaches.

Activating full-disk encryption or file-based encryption protects stored data from unauthorized access in the event of device loss or theft. Utilizing strong passwords, biometric authentication (e.g., fingerprint or facial recognition), or passphrase-based security measures enhances user verification processes and safeguards sensitive information stored on mobile devices from exploitation by malicious actors or unauthorized entities.

Backing Up Mobile Data and Implementing Disaster Recovery Plans

Creating regular backups of mobile data ensures data resilience and facilitates timely recovery in the event of malware infections, device failures, or data loss incidents.

Utilizing cloud-based backup services or synchronizing mobile device data with secure storage repositories enables seamless restoration of critical information and minimizes disruptions to personal or business operations.

Developing and implementing disaster recovery plans, including backup restoration procedures and contingency measures, reinforces preparedness for unexpected events and enhances mobile device resilience against potential security threats or operational disruptions.

Educating Users on Mobile Security Best Practices

Promoting awareness of mobile security best practices among users is essential in cultivating a proactive approach to mobile device protection and minimizing risks associated with malware infections or cyber attacks. Educating users on recognizing suspicious app behaviors, identifying potential security threats, and adhering to established security guidelines empowers them to make informed decisions and adopt preventive measures to safeguard personal or organizational data. Conducting regular security awareness training, disseminating mobile security tips, and encouraging proactive security behaviors contribute to enhancing overall mobile device security posture and resilience against evolving cyber threats.

Collaborative Efforts in Mobile Security

Securing mobile devices against malware requires collaborative efforts among mobile device manufacturers, software developers, cybersecurity experts, and end users to address emerging threats and implement effective security measures. Participating in industry forums, sharing threat intelligence, and adhering to industry standards or regulatory requirements promote collective efforts in enhancing mobile device security frameworks, mitigating risks associated with mobile malware, and fostering a safer digital environment for mobile device users worldwide.

Conclusion

In conclusion, securing mobile devices against malware is paramount for protecting sensitive data, preserving user privacy, and ensuring uninterrupted mobile device functionality in today's interconnected world.

By implementing proactive security measures, maintaining software updates, deploying reputable mobile security solutions, and promoting user awareness of mobile security best practices, individuals and organizations can mitigate risks associated with mobile malware infections and safeguard against potential cyber threats.

Embracing a holistic approach to mobile security, fostering collaboration across sectors, and investing in resilient security strategies empower stakeholders to navigate digital challenges confidently and sustainably, preserving the integrity and confidentiality of mobile device operations and data assets.

Chapter 21: Understanding Ransomware and Strategies for Protection

In the digital age, where connectivity and data are paramount, the threat of ransomware looms large. Ransomware is a malicious software designed to block access to a computer system or files until a sum of money, often in cryptocurrency like Bitcoin, is paid. It has evolved into one of the most lucrative forms of cybercrime, targeting individuals, businesses, and even government institutions worldwide.

What is Ransomware?

Ransomware operates by encrypting files on a victim's computer or network, rendering them inaccessible without a decryption key held by the attacker. It typically spreads through phishing emails, malicious attachments, or exploit kits that take advantage of vulnerabilities in software. Once infected, the ransomware displays a ransom note demanding payment in exchange for the decryption key.

The impact of ransomware can be devastating. It disrupts operations, causes financial losses, damages reputation, and compromises sensitive data. High-profile incidents have highlighted its destructive potential, underscoring the need for robust defenses against such threats.

Types of Ransomware

Ransomware comes in various forms, each with distinct characteristics and methods of operation. **Encrypting ransomware** encrypts files, making them inaccessible until a ransom is paid. **Locker ransomware** locks users out of their devices completely. **Master boot record (MBR) ransomware** infects the MBR of a computer, preventing it from booting up. Each type requires specific countermeasures for mitigation.

Understanding the Attack Vector

Understanding how ransomware infiltrates systems is crucial for prevention. Common vectors include:

1. Phishing Emails: Attackers send emails with malicious attachments or links, tricking recipients into downloading ransomware.

2. Vulnerabilities: Exploiting weaknesses in software or operating systems allows ransomware to gain entry.

3. Malvertising: Malicious advertisements on legitimate websites can lead users to inadvertently download ransomware.

4. Remote Desktop Protocol (RDP) Exploits: Attackers exploit weak RDP configurations to gain unauthorized access to systems.

Protecting Against Ransomware

Mitigating the risk of ransomware involves a multi-faceted approach that integrates technological solutions, user education, and proactive security measures:

1. Regular Backups: Maintain secure, up-to-date backups of critical data. Ensure backups are stored offline or in a separate, secure environment to prevent them from being encrypted by ransomware.

2. Endpoint Protection: Deploy robust antivirus and antimalware software across all devices. Ensure they are regularly updated to detect and neutralize ransomware threats.

3. Patch Management: Promptly apply security patches and updates to operating systems, software, and applications. Vulnerabilities are often exploited by ransomware to gain access.

4. Email Security: Implement email filtering and educate users about recognizing phishing attempts. Discourage opening attachments or clicking on links from unknown or suspicious sources.

5. Network Segmentation: Divide networks into segments to contain the spread of ransomware in case of an infection. Restrict user access based on the principle of least privilege.

6. Security Awareness Training: Educate employees about cybersecurity best practices, including identifying phishing attempts and avoiding risky online behavior.

7. Incident Response Plan: Develop and regularly test an incident response plan to quickly identify, contain, and mitigate the impact of ransomware attacks. Ensure key personnel are trained to respond effectively.

8. Encryption and Authentication: Use strong encryption methods to protect sensitive data. Implement multi-factor authentication (MFA) to enhance access control and prevent unauthorized entry.

9. Monitoring and Detection: Deploy intrusion detection systems (IDS) and security information and event management (SIEM) solutions to monitor network activity for signs of ransomware and other threats.

Case Studies and Lessons Learned

Examining real-world ransomware incidents provides valuable insights into evolving tactics and the importance of preparedness. From WannaCry to NotPetya, each incident underscores the critical need for vigilance, timely updates, and a proactive security posture.

Conclusion

As ransomware continues to evolve in sophistication and impact, organizations and individuals must remain vigilant and proactive in their defense strategies.

By implementing a combination of robust cybersecurity practices, user education, and technological defenses, the risk posed by ransomware can be significantly mitigated. Remember, preparation and prevention are key to safeguarding against this pervasive cyber threat.

Chapter 22: The Role of VPNs in Protecting Your Privacy

In an era dominated by digital connectivity and online interactions, concerns about privacy and data security have become increasingly paramount. Virtual Private Networks (VPNs) have emerged as essential tools for individuals and organizations seeking to safeguard their sensitive information from prying eyes and malicious actors. This chapter explores the fundamental role of VPNs in protecting privacy, their mechanisms of operation, benefits, considerations, and practical applications.

Understanding VPNs

A VPN establishes a secure, encrypted connection between a user's device and a remote server operated by the VPN service provider.

This encrypted tunnel shields data transmitted over the internet from interception or surveillance by third parties, including hackers, government agencies, or internet service providers (ISPs).

By routing internet traffic through this encrypted tunnel, VPNs effectively mask the user's IP address and geographic location, enhancing anonymity and privacy online.

Mechanisms of Operation

When a user initiates a VPN connection, their device encrypts all outgoing data before sending it to the VPN server. The VPN server decrypts the data and forwards it to the intended destination on the internet. Responses from the destination are encrypted by the VPN server before being sent back to the user's device. This encryption-decryption process ensures that data transmitted over the VPN remains secure and private, even on unsecured or public Wi-Fi networks.

Privacy Benefits of VPNs

1. **IP Address Masking:** VPNs replace the user's real IP address with one from the VPN server's pool of addresses. This prevents websites, advertisers, or malicious actors from identifying the user's actual geographic location.
2. **Encryption:** VPNs encrypt data using robust encryption protocols (such as AES-256), making it unreadable to anyone intercepting it. This protects sensitive information such as passwords, credit card details, and personal communications.
3. **Anonymous Browsing:** By hiding the user's IP address and encrypting their internet traffic, VPNs enable anonymous browsing

and prevent tracking by websites and online services.

4. **Access Control:** VPNs allow users to bypass geographic restrictions and censorship by accessing websites and online services that may be blocked in their region.

Considerations When Choosing a VPN

Not all VPN services are created equal. When selecting a VPN provider, consider the following factors:

- **Encryption Strength:** Ensure the VPN uses strong encryption protocols, such as AES-256, to protect your data.
- **No-Logs Policy:** Choose a VPN provider that adheres to a strict no-logs policy, meaning they do not store records of your online activity or connection logs.
- **Server Locations:** Evaluate the VPN provider's server locations and ensure they offer servers in countries where you need to access content or services.
- **Speed and Reliability:** Test the VPN for speed and reliability, especially if you need to stream content or perform data-intensive activities.
- **Compatibility:** Ensure the VPN is compatible with all your devices and operating systems,

including desktop computers, smartphones, and tablets.

Practical Applications of VPNs

VPNs are versatile tools with various practical applications:

- **Remote Work:** VPNs enable secure access to corporate networks and confidential information when working remotely.
- **Public Wi-Fi Security:** Protect sensitive data from interception on public Wi-Fi networks, such as those in cafes, airports, or hotels.
- **Privacy While Traveling:** Maintain privacy and access geo-blocked content while traveling abroad by connecting to VPN servers in your home country.
- **Torrenting and P2P Sharing:** VPNs provide anonymity and security when downloading torrents or engaging in peer-to-peer file sharing activities.

VPNs and Digital Privacy Legislation

As global awareness of digital privacy issues grows, governments are implementing stricter regulations governing data protection and privacy. VPNs play a crucial role in complying with these regulations by safeguarding user data from unauthorized access and surveillance.

Conclusion

In conclusion, VPNs are indispensable tools for protecting digital privacy in an increasingly interconnected world. By encrypting internet traffic, masking IP addresses, and providing anonymous browsing capabilities, VPNs empower individuals and organizations to safeguard sensitive information from cyber threats and intrusive surveillance.

When selecting a VPN provider, prioritize factors such as encryption strength, privacy policies, and compatibility to ensure comprehensive protection of your online activities and data privacy. As technology continues to evolve, VPNs will remain essential allies in the ongoing battle for digital privacy and security.

Chapter 23: Avoiding Fake Antivirus Scams

In the realm of cybersecurity threats, fake antivirus scams stand out as particularly insidious. These scams prey on users' fears of malware and cyberattacks, presenting themselves as legitimate antivirus software promising protection and security. However, instead of safeguarding computers, these fake antivirus programs often deceive users into paying for useless software, compromising their personal information, or even infecting their systems with real malware. Understanding how these scams operate, recognizing their red flags, and adopting preventive measures are crucial steps in protecting oneself from falling victim.

How Fake Antivirus Scams Operate

Fake antivirus scams typically begin with deceptive advertisements or malicious websites claiming to offer free antivirus scans or urgent alerts about supposed security threats. Upon visiting such sites, users may encounter pop-up messages warning of malware infections detected on their systems. These messages often employ scare tactics, urging immediate action to remove the alleged threats.

In some cases, users are prompted to download and install a software application purportedly capable of detecting and removing the reported malware. This software may appear convincing, mimicking the interface and branding of legitimate antivirus products. Once installed, the fake antivirus program may perform a superficial scan, displaying fabricated or exaggerated results to further alarm the user.

To "resolve" the reported issues, users are typically prompted to purchase a full version of the fake antivirus software or subscribe to a service promising ongoing protection. Payments are often requested via credit card or other online payment methods, facilitating financial exploitation of victims.

Recognizing Red Flags

Recognizing the warning signs of fake antivirus scams can help users avoid falling prey to these deceptive tactics:

1. **Unsolicited Pop-up Alerts:** Be cautious of unexpected pop-up messages or browser redirects warning of malware infections, especially when browsing unfamiliar websites or clicking on suspicious links.
2. **High-Pressure Tactics:** Scammers use urgency and fear to manipulate victims into

immediate action. Genuine antivirus software does not pressure users with urgent warnings demanding instant payment or installation.

3. **Unsolicited Downloads:** Avoid downloading software from unfamiliar websites or links embedded in unsolicited emails. Verify the legitimacy of antivirus software by visiting the official website of reputable security vendors.

4. **Poor Website Design and Grammar:** Fake antivirus websites often exhibit poor design, spelling errors, or grammatical mistakes. Legitimate security vendors maintain professional websites with clear, accurate information.

5. **No Known Publisher:** Check the publisher's details and user reviews before downloading antivirus software. Legitimate products are typically well-known, with established reputations and positive feedback from users.

Protecting Against Fake Antivirus Scams

Implementing proactive measures can help safeguard against falling victim to fake antivirus scams:

- **Use Reputable Antivirus Software:** Install and regularly update antivirus software from well-known, trusted vendors. Genuine antivirus programs provide real-time protection against malware and security threats.

- **Verify Sources:** Download software only from official websites of reputable vendors or trusted app stores. Avoid clicking on links or downloading attachments from unknown or suspicious sources.
- **Enable Pop-up Blockers:** Configure web browsers to block pop-up windows, reducing the risk of encountering deceptive advertisements or scareware tactics.
- **Educate Yourself and Others:** Stay informed about common cybersecurity threats, including fake antivirus scams. Educate family members, friends, and colleagues about recognizing and avoiding potential scams.
- **Regular Software Updates:** Keep operating systems, browsers, and software applications up to date with the latest security patches and updates. Vulnerabilities in outdated software can be exploited by scammers to deliver fake antivirus programs or malware.

Responding to Suspected Scams

If you suspect that you have encountered a fake antivirus scam or installed fraudulent software:

- **Disconnect from the Internet:** Immediately disconnect your device from the internet to prevent further communication with potentially malicious servers or websites.
- **Uninstall Suspicious Software:** Remove any suspicious software or applications from your device using the standard uninstallation process. Consult the official support resources of your operating system or antivirus vendor for guidance.
- **Run a Full System Scan:** Perform a comprehensive scan of your computer using reputable antivirus software to detect and remove any malware or potentially unwanted programs (PUPs) that may have been installed.
- **Monitor Financial Accounts:** Monitor your bank accounts and credit card statements for unauthorized transactions. If you provided payment information to a suspected scam, contact your financial institution to report potential fraud and take appropriate action.

Reporting Scams

Reporting fake antivirus scams and other cybersecurity threats can help protect others and facilitate enforcement actions:

- **Internet Crime Complaint Center (IC3):** Report suspected internet crime, including fake antivirus scams, to the IC3, a partnership between the FBI and the National White Collar Crime Center.
- **Federal Trade Commission (FTC):** File a complaint with the FTC, which works to protect consumers from fraudulent and deceptive practices.
- **Local Authorities:** Contact local law enforcement or consumer protection agencies to report scams targeting residents in your area.

Conclusion

In conclusion, awareness and vigilance are essential defenses against fake antivirus scams. By understanding how these scams operate, recognizing red flags, and adopting proactive measures to protect against them, users can minimize the risk of falling victim to deceptive tactics aimed at exploiting fears of cyber threats.

Staying informed, using reputable antivirus software, and exercising caution when browsing online are critical steps in maintaining cybersecurity and safeguarding personal information from malicious actors seeking to exploit vulnerabilities for financial gain.

Chapter 24: Regularly Scanning Your Computer for Malware

In today's interconnected digital world, the threat of malware looms large over computer users, businesses, and organizations alike. Malware, short for malicious software, encompasses a wide range of malicious programs designed to infiltrate, damage, or gain unauthorized access to computer systems and networks. Regularly scanning your computer for malware is a fundamental practice in cybersecurity, crucial for identifying and mitigating threats before they can cause significant harm. This chapter explores the importance of malware scanning, effective scanning techniques, recommended tools, and proactive measures to enhance computer security.

Understanding Malware and Its Threats

Malware encompasses various types, each designed with specific malicious intent. **Viruses** attach themselves to legitimate programs and spread when those programs are executed. **Trojans** masquerade as legitimate software to trick users into installing them, often enabling remote access or data theft. **Ransomware** encrypts files and demands ransom for decryption. **Spyware** secretly gathers information about a user's activities.

Worms replicate themselves to spread across networks, causing widespread damage.

The impact of malware can be devastating, ranging from data breaches and financial losses to operational disruptions and reputational damage. As malware continues to evolve in sophistication and prevalence, regular scanning of computer systems becomes essential to detect and mitigate potential threats promptly.

Importance of Regular Malware Scanning

Regular malware scanning forms a critical component of proactive cybersecurity practices for several reasons:

1. **Early Detection:** Detecting malware early minimizes its potential impact, preventing data loss, system corruption, and unauthorized access.
2. **Preventive Maintenance:** Regular scanning helps maintain the health and performance of computer systems by identifying and removing harmful programs that could degrade system performance or compromise stability.
3. **Compliance Requirements:** Many industries and regulatory standards mandate regular malware scanning as part of data protection

and compliance measures to safeguard sensitive information.

4. **Peace of Mind:** Knowing that your computer is regularly scanned for malware provides peace of mind, allowing users to browse the internet, download files, and conduct online transactions with greater confidence.

Effective Malware Scanning Techniques

Effective malware scanning involves employing comprehensive techniques to thoroughly examine computer systems for signs of malicious activity:

1. **Scheduled Scans:** Schedule regular scans of your computer using reputable antivirus or anti-malware software. Set scans to run during periods when the computer is typically idle to minimize disruption.
2. **Full System Scans:** Conduct full system scans periodically to thoroughly examine all files, programs, and system areas for malware. Full scans ensure comprehensive coverage, including hidden or deeply embedded threats.
3. **Custom Scans:** Perform custom scans targeting specific files, folders, or areas of concern identified through suspicious behavior, unusual system performance, or security alerts.

4. **Real-Time Protection:** Enable real-time scanning and proactive detection features offered by antivirus software to detect and block malware in real-time as it attempts to infiltrate the system.
5. **Behavioral Analysis:** Utilize antivirus solutions equipped with behavioral analysis capabilities to identify and block malware based on suspicious behaviors or patterns, even if the malware's signature is unknown.

Recommended Tools and Software

Selecting reputable antivirus or anti-malware software is crucial for effective malware scanning and protection:

- **Antivirus Software:** Choose antivirus software from well-established vendors known for reliable detection rates, regular updates, and comprehensive protection against a wide range of malware threats.
- **Anti-Malware Tools:** Supplement antivirus protection with specialized anti-malware tools designed to detect and remove specific types of malware, such as spyware, adware, or ransomware.
- **Firewall Protection:** Implement firewall protection to monitor and control incoming and outgoing network traffic, preventing

unauthorized access and blocking malicious communication attempts.
- **Browser Extensions:** Install browser extensions or add-ons that enhance security by blocking malicious websites, preventing phishing attacks, and scanning downloaded files for malware.

Proactive Measures for Enhanced Security

In addition to regular malware scanning, adopt proactive measures to strengthen overall computer security:

- **Keep Software Updated:** Maintain up-to-date operating systems, software applications, and antivirus definitions to patch security vulnerabilities exploited by malware.
- **Exercise Caution Online:** Practice safe browsing habits by avoiding suspicious websites, clicking on unknown links, or downloading files from untrusted sources.
- **Backup Data Regularly:** Implement a regular backup regimen to store copies of important files and data securely, protecting against data loss caused by malware infections or ransomware attacks.
- **User Education:** Educate yourself and others about cybersecurity best practices, including recognizing phishing attempts, avoiding

social engineering tactics, and securely managing passwords.

Conclusion

Regularly scanning your computer for malware is a fundamental practice in maintaining cybersecurity and protecting against the ever-present threat of malicious software.

By understanding the types of malware, recognizing the importance of regular scanning, employing effective scanning techniques, and using reputable security tools, users can significantly reduce the risk of malware infections and their associated consequences.

Embrace a proactive approach to computer security by implementing regular scans, adopting recommended tools and software, and reinforcing security measures to safeguard personal and organizational data from evolving cyber threats. Remember, proactive prevention is key to maintaining a resilient defense against malware and ensuring a secure computing environment.

Chapter 25: Securing Your Home Network

In the modern digital age, the home network serves as the backbone of connectivity, enabling households to access the internet, share resources, and connect multiple devices seamlessly. However, with this convenience comes the responsibility of ensuring the security and integrity of the home network. Securing your home network is essential to protect sensitive information, prevent unauthorized access, and safeguard against cyber threats. This chapter explores practical strategies, best practices, and essential tools to strengthen the security of your home network effectively.

Understanding the Home Network Landscape

A typical home network consists of several interconnected devices, including computers, smartphones, tablets, smart TVs, gaming consoles, and IoT (Internet of Things) devices such as smart thermostats and security cameras. These devices communicate with each other and the internet through a router, which serves as the gateway between the home network and the broader online world.

Steps to Secure Your Home Network

1. **Change Default Router Settings:** Begin by accessing your router's administrative interface using the default IP address and login credentials provided by the manufacturer. Change the default username and password to a strong, unique combination to prevent unauthorized access.
2. **Update Router Firmware:** Regularly check for and install firmware updates provided by the router manufacturer. Firmware updates often include security patches and enhancements to protect against vulnerabilities exploited by cyber attackers.
3. **Enable Network Encryption:** Protect your wireless network by enabling WPA3 (Wi-Fi Protected Access 3) or WPA2 encryption. Avoid using outdated encryption standards like WEP (Wired Equivalent Privacy), which are vulnerable to security breaches.
4. **Secure Wireless Network Settings:** Disable SSID (Service Set Identifier) broadcasting to prevent your network name from being broadcasted publicly. Use a unique and strong SSID that does not reveal personal information or the router's make/model.
5. **Implement Strong Passwords:** Create strong, complex passwords for your Wi-Fi network and all devices connected to it. Use a combination of uppercase and lowercase

letters, numbers, and special characters to enhance password strength.

6. **Use Guest Networks:** Configure a separate guest network for visitors to use, isolated from your main network. Guest networks restrict access to your devices and data while allowing guests to access the internet.

7. **Enable Firewall Protection:** Activate the built-in firewall feature on your router to monitor incoming and outgoing network traffic. Configure firewall settings to block suspicious or unauthorized access attempts.

8. **Disable UPnP (Universal Plug and Play):** UPnP can pose security risks by automatically opening ports on your router, potentially exposing your network to unauthorized access. Disable UPnP unless necessary for specific applications.

9. **Limit Device Access:** Restrict access to your network by MAC (Media Access Control) address filtering. Configure your router to only allow specific devices with known MAC addresses to connect to the network.

10. **Monitor Connected Devices:** Regularly review the list of devices connected to your network through the router's administrative interface. Remove any unrecognized or unauthorized devices to prevent unauthorized access.

Securing IoT Devices

IoT devices, such as smart home appliances and devices, present unique security challenges due to their often limited security features and continuous connectivity:

- **Change Default Passwords:** Immediately change default passwords on IoT devices to strong, unique passwords. Avoid using default credentials provided by manufacturers.
- **Update Firmware:** Regularly check for firmware updates for IoT devices and install updates promptly to patch security vulnerabilities.
- **Segment IoT Devices:** Separate IoT devices into their own network segment or VLAN (Virtual Local Area Network) to isolate them from your main network and limit their impact in case of a compromise.
- **Monitor Device Activity:** Monitor the behavior and network activity of IoT devices for unusual or suspicious activity that may indicate a security breach.

Additional Security Measures

- **Use Antivirus and Security Software:** Install reputable antivirus software on all devices connected to your home network, including computers, smartphones, and tablets. Keep antivirus definitions up to date to protect against malware threats.

- **Enable Two-Factor Authentication (2FA):** Enable 2FA for accounts associated with your home network, router, and IoT devices. 2FA adds an extra layer of security by requiring a second form of verification in addition to a password.
- **Educate Family Members:** Educate household members about cybersecurity best practices, including recognizing phishing attempts, avoiding suspicious links, and practicing safe internet and device usage habits.
- **Backup Important Data:** Implement a regular backup strategy to store copies of critical data and files securely. Backups protect against data loss caused by malware infections, hardware failures, or ransomware attacks.

Conclusion

Securing your home network is essential to protect your privacy, personal information, and connected devices from evolving cyber threats.

By understanding the home network landscape, implementing proactive security measures, and staying informed about cybersecurity best practices, you can create a resilient defense against unauthorized access, malware infections, and other potential risks.

Regularly review and update your network security settings, monitor device activity, and educate household members to maintain a secure and reliable home network environment. Remember, proactive prevention and vigilance are key to safeguarding your digital assets and ensuring a safe online experience for everyone in your household.

Chapter 26: Understanding and Using Browser Security Settings

In today's digital age, where much of our lives unfold online, ensuring the security of our browsing activities is paramount. Browser security settings play a crucial role in safeguarding our privacy, protecting against malicious attacks, and maintaining the integrity of our personal data. This chapter delves into the intricacies of these settings, guiding you through their importance, functionality, and practical application.

Importance of Browser Security Settings

Browser security settings serve as the first line of defense against a myriad of online threats, ranging from phishing scams to malware infections. By configuring these settings correctly, users can mitigate risks associated with unauthorized access, data breaches, and identity theft. Understanding their significance involves recognizing the vulnerabilities inherent in internet browsing and acknowledging the proactive measures needed to counteract them.

Key Components of Browser Security

1. **Privacy Settings**: Central to browser security, privacy settings allow users to control how

their browsing data is collected, stored, and shared. This includes managing cookies, which are small pieces of data stored on your computer by websites to track your activities.

Modern browsers offer granular controls over cookies, enabling users to block third-party cookies, clear browsing history, and set preferences for handling location data. Such measures not only enhance privacy but also reduce the likelihood of targeted advertising and tracking.

2. **Security Certificates and HTTPS**: Security certificates, indicated by HTTPS in the browser's address bar, signify encrypted connections between your device and websites. This encryption prevents unauthorized interception of data transmitted over the internet, safeguarding sensitive information such as login credentials and financial details.

   Users should verify the presence of HTTPS and security certificates when entering personal information or conducting financial transactions online. Browsers often provide warnings when attempting to access sites without valid certificates, underscoring the importance of secure connections in maintaining data integrity.

3. **Pop-up and Content Blockers**: Pop-ups and malicious content can pose significant security risks by potentially exposing users to malware or deceptive websites. Browser settings allow for the blocking of pop-ups and unwanted content, thereby mitigating these risks and preserving the browsing experience.

   Effective use of pop-up blockers involves configuring settings to selectively allow pop-ups from trusted sites while blocking those deemed intrusive or harmful. This proactive approach minimizes distractions and protects against inadvertent exposure to malicious content.

Configuring Browser Security Settings

Navigating browser security settings involves a series of intuitive steps tailored to each browser's interface and functionality. The following guidelines outline essential practices for configuring these settings effectively:

1. **Accessing Settings**: Begin by locating the browser's settings menu, typically accessible through an icon resembling three vertical

dots or lines in the upper-right corner of the window. Clicking on this icon reveals a dropdown menu containing options to access settings, extensions, and additional tools.

2. **Privacy and Security**: Within the settings menu, locate the section dedicated to privacy and security preferences. Here, users can customize settings related to cookies, site permissions, and data collection practices. Adjusting these preferences according to personal comfort levels ensures a balance between privacy protection and functional convenience.

3. **Updating Browser Versions**: Regularly updating browser software is critical for incorporating security patches and enhancements designed to address emerging threats. Automated updates streamline this process by ensuring that the latest security measures are applied promptly, thereby fortifying defenses against evolving cyber risks.

4. **Extension Management**: Extensions and add-ons extend the functionality of browsers but may also introduce security vulnerabilities if improperly configured or sourced from unverified developers. Prioritize installing extensions from reputable sources and regularly review their

permissions and access privileges to minimize potential risks.

Enhancing Browser Security: Best Practices

Achieving robust browser security extends beyond configuration settings to encompass proactive habits and informed decision-making:

1. **Password Management**: Adopting strong, unique passwords for each online account reduces the likelihood of unauthorized access in the event of a security breach. Consider utilizing password managers to securely store and generate complex passwords, enhancing overall account security.
2. **Two-Factor Authentication (2FA)**: Enable two-factor authentication wherever possible to add an extra layer of security beyond passwords. This supplementary measure typically involves receiving a verification code via SMS or authentication apps, further securing access to sensitive accounts.
3. **Regular Security Audits**: Conduct periodic audits of browser settings, extensions, and saved credentials to identify and address potential security vulnerabilities. Maintaining vigilance and promptly addressing any suspicious activity or unauthorized access enhances overall cybersecurity posture.

Conclusion

Mastering browser security settings entails a blend of knowledge, vigilance, and proactive engagement with evolving digital threats. By prioritizing privacy, embracing encryption protocols, and adhering to best practices, users can navigate the internet confidently while safeguarding their personal information and digital assets. Empowered with these insights, you are equipped to harness the full potential of browser security settings, fostering a safer and more secure online experience.

Chapter 27: Risks of Using Public Wi-Fi and How to Mitigate Them

In an increasingly interconnected world, public Wi-Fi networks have become ubiquitous, offering convenient internet access in cafes, airports, hotels, and other public spaces. While these networks provide immediate connectivity, they also introduce significant security risks that can compromise sensitive data and personal information. This chapter explores the inherent dangers of using public Wi-Fi and outlines effective strategies for mitigating these risks to safeguard your digital privacy.

Understanding the Risks

Public Wi-Fi networks, often unsecured and accessible to anyone within range, present several vulnerabilities that malicious actors can exploit:

1. Man-in-the-Middle Attacks: One of the most common threats associated with public Wi-Fi is the risk of man-in-the-middle (MitM) attacks. In this scenario, hackers intercept communication between your device and the network, allowing them to eavesdrop on sensitive information such as login credentials, financial transactions, and personal messages.

2. Malware Distribution: Public Wi-Fi networks may serve as conduits for malware distribution, where attackers inject malicious software into unsuspecting users' devices. This malware can compromise device security, steal data, or even enable remote control of the device without the user's knowledge.

3. Rogue Networks and Spoofing: Cybercriminals can set up rogue Wi-Fi networks with legitimate-sounding names to deceive users into connecting. Known as spoofing, this tactic enables attackers to monitor internet traffic, capture login credentials, and distribute malware under the guise of a trusted network.

4. Snooping and Data Interception: Unencrypted data transmitted over public Wi-Fi networks is vulnerable to interception by nearby eavesdroppers. This includes sensitive information transmitted via unsecured websites or applications, exposing users to identity theft, fraud, and unauthorized access to personal accounts.

Mitigating Public Wi-Fi Risks

To mitigate the risks associated with public Wi-Fi usage and safeguard your digital security, adopt the following proactive measures:

1. Use a Virtual Private Network (VPN): Employing a VPN encrypts your internet traffic, creating a secure tunnel between your device and a VPN server. This encryption prevents unauthorized interception of data, shielding sensitive information from potential eavesdroppers and MitM attacks. Choose reputable VPN services that prioritize privacy and adhere to strict security protocols.

2. Verify Network Authenticity: Before connecting to a public Wi-Fi network, verify its authenticity by confirming the network name and ensuring it is provided by a legitimate source, such as the establishment's official network. Avoid connecting to networks with generic or suspicious names to mitigate the risk of falling victim to spoofing attacks.

3. Enable Firewall Protection: Activate firewall protection on your device to monitor and filter incoming and outgoing network traffic. Firewalls act as barriers against unauthorized access attempts and suspicious activities, enhancing overall defense against malware and intrusive network threats.

4. Avoid Sensitive Transactions: Refrain from conducting sensitive transactions, such as online banking or entering credit card information, while connected to public Wi-Fi networks. If conducting essential tasks, ensure the website uses HTTPS encryption and consider using a VPN for additional security layers.

5. Update Software and Applications: Keep your device's operating system, web browsers, and applications up to date with the latest security patches and updates. Regular updates address vulnerabilities exploited by cybercriminals and strengthen overall device security against emerging threats.

6. Use Two-Factor Authentication (2FA): Enable two-factor authentication (2FA) on accounts that support it to add an extra layer of security beyond passwords. This supplementary measure requires a second form of verification, such as a code sent to your mobile device, reducing the risk of unauthorized access even if login credentials are compromised.

7. Disable Auto-Connect Features: Disable auto-connect features on your device to prevent automatic connection to open or previously used Wi-Fi networks. Manual connection allows you to scrutinize network security settings and make informed decisions before accessing potentially risky networks.

Educating Others and Promoting Awareness

In addition to safeguarding your personal digital security, educate others about the risks associated with public Wi-Fi usage and share best practices for mitigating these risks. Promote awareness of VPN usage, network verification techniques, and the importance of updating software to collectively enhance cybersecurity preparedness across diverse user communities.

Conclusion

Navigating the risks of public Wi-Fi networks requires a combination of vigilance, knowledge, and proactive security measures. By understanding the vulnerabilities inherent in public Wi-Fi usage and implementing effective mitigation strategies such as VPN adoption, network verification, and software updates, users can safeguard their digital privacy and protect sensitive information from malicious exploitation.

Empowered with these insights, you are equipped to make informed decisions when accessing public Wi-Fi networks, fostering a safer and more secure online experience in today's interconnected landscape.

Chapter 28: Parental Controls and Protecting Kids Online

In an era where digital interactions are integral to daily life, children are increasingly exposed to the vast and often unfiltered landscape of the internet. While the online world offers educational resources, entertainment, and social connectivity, it also harbors potential risks and inappropriate content that may impact young minds. This chapter explores the importance of parental controls in managing children's online activities and provides strategies for fostering a safe and positive digital environment.

Understanding the Digital Landscape for Children

Children today navigate a digital landscape characterized by limitless information access, social media platforms, online gaming communities, and interactive content. While these digital resources offer opportunities for learning and creativity, they also pose inherent risks such as exposure to explicit content, cyberbullying, online predators, and addictive behaviors. Parents play a pivotal role in guiding their children's digital experiences, equipping them with the necessary tools and knowledge to navigate safely and responsibly online.

The Role of Parental Controls

Parental controls encompass a range of tools and strategies designed to monitor and manage children's online activities effectively. These controls enable parents to establish boundaries, enforce age-appropriate content restrictions, and mitigate potential risks associated with internet usage. Key features of parental control solutions include:

1. Content Filtering: Parental control software allows parents to filter web content based on predefined categories such as violence, adult content, gambling, and more. This filtering mechanism helps shield children from exposure to inappropriate material while promoting a safer browsing experience.

2. Time Management: Managing screen time is essential in balancing online activities with other aspects of a child's life, such as academics, physical activity, and social interactions. Parental controls enable parents to set time limits for device usage, schedule internet access periods, and establish bedtime restrictions to promote healthy digital habits.

3. App and Game Controls: With the proliferation of mobile apps and online games, parental controls offer features to regulate access to specific applications and gaming platforms. Parents can block or restrict downloads of apps based on age ratings, monitor in-app purchases, and manage gameplay duration to prevent excessive screen time.

4. Privacy and Social Media Monitoring: Monitoring children's social media interactions and online communications is crucial for safeguarding their privacy and protecting against cyberbullying or predatory behavior. Parental control tools provide insights into social media activity, messaging content, and friend lists, empowering parents to intervene proactively when necessary.

Implementing Effective Parental Controls

When implementing parental controls to protect children online, consider the following best practices and strategies:

1. Open Communication: Foster open and ongoing communication with children about internet safety, digital citizenship, and responsible online behavior. Establishing trust and encouraging dialogue empowers children to seek guidance when encountering unfamiliar or concerning online content.

2. Customize Settings: Tailor parental control settings to align with children's age, maturity level, and individual needs. Adjust content filters, time restrictions, and monitoring parameters to strike a balance between protection and age-appropriate independence in online activities.

3. Educate Yourself: Stay informed about popular websites, social media trends, online gaming platforms, and digital applications frequented by children.

Understanding these digital landscapes equips parents with insights into potential risks and opportunities to engage in constructive conversations with their children.

4. Monitor Effectively: Regularly review parental control reports and activity logs to assess children's online behavior, identify emerging trends or concerns, and adjust settings as needed. Monitoring provides visibility into internet usage patterns and facilitates informed discussions about online safety practices.

5. Respect Privacy: While monitoring children's online activities is essential for their safety, respect their privacy by discussing the purpose and parameters of parental controls openly. Encourage mutual understanding and collaborative decision-making to promote a supportive and respectful digital environment.

Promoting Digital Literacy and Responsible Citizenship

Beyond implementing technical safeguards, promoting digital literacy and responsible citizenship empowers children to navigate online challenges with confidence and integrity. Encourage critical thinking skills, media literacy, and ethical digital practices through educational initiatives, family discussions, and interactive learning experiences. By nurturing a positive digital mindset, children develop resilience, empathy, and informed decision-making skills essential for thriving in the digital age.

Conclusion

Parental controls serve as invaluable tools in safeguarding children's online experiences, mitigating risks, and promoting responsible digital citizenship. By leveraging content filtering, time management features, and proactive monitoring, parents can create a supportive digital environment that prioritizes safety, privacy, and healthy screen habits.

Coupled with open communication, education on internet safety, and fostering digital literacy, parental controls empower families to navigate the complexities of the online world with confidence and resilience. Together, these strategies cultivate a balanced approach to managing children's online activities, ensuring they harness the benefits of technology while navigating potential risks effectively.

Chapter 29: Recognizing Social Engineering Attacks

In the realm of cybersecurity, social engineering stands as a formidable tactic employed by malicious actors to exploit human psychology and manipulate individuals into divulging sensitive information or performing actions that compromise security. Unlike traditional hacking methods that target technical vulnerabilities, social engineering attacks leverage deception, trust manipulation, and psychological manipulation to achieve their objectives. This chapter explores various types of social engineering attacks, common tactics employed by attackers, and strategies for recognizing and mitigating these deceptive threats.

Understanding Social Engineering

Social engineering encompasses a range of deceptive techniques used to exploit human behavior and trust to gain unauthorized access to sensitive information, systems, or physical spaces. Unlike automated attacks that exploit software vulnerabilities, social engineering relies on interpersonal skills, manipulation, and psychological tactics to achieve malicious goals. Attackers exploit inherent human traits such as curiosity, fear, and willingness to help, making social engineering attacks highly effective and challenging to detect.

Types of Social Engineering Attacks

1. **Phishing:** Phishing remains one of the most prevalent and widespread forms of social engineering attacks. Attackers impersonate trusted entities, such as legitimate companies or organizations, and lure victims into clicking malicious links, downloading infected attachments, or disclosing confidential information such as login credentials, financial details, or personal data.

2. **Spear Phishing:** Spear phishing targets specific individuals or organizations, tailoring deceptive messages with personalized information to increase credibility and manipulate victims into taking desired actions. Attackers conduct thorough reconnaissance to gather personal details, interests, and relationships, enhancing the authenticity and effectiveness of spear phishing campaigns.

3. **Baiting:** Baiting involves enticing victims with promises of rewards or benefits, such as free downloads, coupons, or physical items, to lure them into compromising security. Attackers distribute infected USB drives, compromised software downloads, or

fake promotions that exploit victims' curiosity or desire for perceived gains.

4. **Pretexting:** Pretexting relies on creating a fabricated scenario or pretext to manipulate victims into divulging confidential information or performing actions that benefit the attacker. Attackers often impersonate authority figures, coworkers, or trusted individuals, exploiting trust and exploiting social norms to gain access to sensitive information.

5. **Quid Pro Quo:** Quid pro quo attacks offer immediate benefits or assistance in exchange for sensitive information or access to systems. Attackers pose as IT support personnel, service providers, or technical experts offering help with software issues or account problems, leveraging victims' willingness to cooperate in exchange for perceived assistance.

Recognizing Indicators of Social Engineering Attacks

Detecting social engineering attacks requires vigilance, critical thinking, and awareness of common indicators and red flags that may signal deceptive tactics:

- **Unsolicited Requests:** Be cautious of unsolicited emails, messages, or phone calls requesting personal information, login credentials, or financial details, especially from unfamiliar or unexpected sources.

- **Sense of Urgency:** Attackers often create a sense of urgency or fear to pressure victims into immediate action, such as threatening consequences for non-compliance or promising limited-time offers to exploit impulsive decisions.
- **Requests for Confidential Information:** Legitimate organizations typically do not request sensitive information such as passwords, Social Security numbers, or financial details via insecure channels or without proper authentication protocols.
- **Unexpected Rewards or Benefits:** Exercise caution when presented with unexpected rewards, free downloads, or lucrative offers that require disclosing personal information or downloading unknown files.
- **Inconsistencies in Communication:** Scrutinize inconsistencies in email addresses, domain names, language use, or formatting errors that indicate fraudulent communications or impersonation attempts.

Strategies for Mitigating Social Engineering Risks

To mitigate the risks posed by social engineering attacks and protect against potential vulnerabilities, consider implementing the following proactive strategies:

- **Employee Training and Awareness:** Educate employees and individuals about common social engineering tactics, red flags, and best practices for securely handling sensitive information and verifying the legitimacy of requests.
- **Implement Multifactor Authentication (MFA):** Implement multifactor authentication (MFA) for accessing systems, applications, and sensitive data to add an additional layer of security beyond passwords, reducing the risk of unauthorized access even if credentials are compromised.
- **Regular Security Assessments:** Conduct regular security assessments, phishing simulations, and vulnerability scans to identify weaknesses in organizational security posture and address potential entry points exploited by social engineering attacks.
- **Use Reliable Security Software:** Deploy reputable antivirus software, firewalls, and intrusion detection systems (IDS) to detect and mitigate suspicious activities, malware infections, or unauthorized access attempts resulting from social engineering attacks.
- **Establish Incident Response Protocols:** Develop and implement incident response

protocols and procedures to promptly address and mitigate the impact of social engineering attacks, including reporting incidents, conducting forensic analysis, and implementing corrective measures.

Conclusion

Recognizing and mitigating social engineering attacks require a proactive approach, informed awareness, and a comprehensive understanding of deceptive tactics employed by malicious actors.

By fostering a culture of cybersecurity awareness, educating individuals about common threats, and implementing robust security measures, organizations and individuals can effectively defend against social engineering attacks and protect sensitive information, systems, and assets.

Vigilance, critical thinking, and ongoing education remain paramount in navigating the evolving landscape of cybersecurity threats and maintaining a resilient defense against social engineering exploits.

Chapter 30: Ensuring Safe Online Shopping and Banking

In the digital age, online shopping and banking have become integral parts of our daily lives, offering convenience and accessibility. However, with this convenience comes the responsibility to ensure our transactions and financial information are secure. This chapter explores essential practices and tips to safeguard yourself while engaging in online shopping and banking.

Understanding the Risks

Before delving into safety measures, it's crucial to understand the risks associated with online transactions. Cybercriminals are adept at exploiting vulnerabilities to steal sensitive information such as credit card details, login credentials, and personal data. Common threats include phishing attacks, malware, insecure Wi-Fi networks, and compromised websites. Recognizing these risks is the first step toward implementing effective protection strategies.

Choosing Secure Websites and Apps

When shopping or banking online, always prioritize security. Ensure the website or mobile app you use is legitimate and reputable. Look for HTTPS in the

URL and a padlock icon in the address bar, indicating a secure connection. Avoid accessing sensitive information through public Wi-Fi networks, as they are more susceptible to interception by hackers.

Strengthening Passwords and Authentication

Strong passwords are your frontline defense against unauthorized access. Create complex passwords using a mix of letters, numbers, and special characters, and avoid using easily guessable information such as birthdays or names. Consider using a password manager to securely store and generate passwords for different accounts. Additionally, enable two-factor authentication (2FA) wherever possible to add an extra layer of security.

Monitoring Financial Statements

Regularly monitor your bank and credit card statements for any unauthorized transactions. Promptly report any suspicious activity to your financial institution to mitigate potential losses. Many banks offer alerts via email or SMS for transactions exceeding a certain amount, providing an early warning system against fraud.

Educating Yourself Against Phishing

Phishing remains one of the most prevalent cyber threats. Attackers masquerade as trustworthy entities through email, text messages, or fake websites to deceive users into revealing sensitive information. Be cautious of unexpected emails requesting personal information or urgent action. Verify the legitimacy of requests by contacting the organization directly through official channels.

Updating Software and Security Measures

Keep your devices, operating systems, and antivirus software up to date to protect against the latest threats. Software updates often include patches for security vulnerabilities identified by developers. Enable automatic updates whenever possible to ensure continuous protection against emerging cyber threats.

Using Secure Payment Methods

When making online purchases, opt for secure payment methods such as credit cards or reputable third-party payment processors like PayPal. These methods offer additional layers of security, such as buyer protection programs and encryption of financial information during transactions. Avoid using debit cards directly for online shopping due to their direct link to your bank account.

Practicing Vigilance with Personal Information

Be mindful of the personal information you share online. Limit the disclosure of sensitive details such as your Social Security number, driver's license, or passport information unless absolutely necessary. Review privacy settings on social media platforms and other online accounts to control who can access your personal information.

Securing Mobile Devices

Mobile devices are increasingly targeted by cybercriminals due to their ubiquity and vulnerabilities. Secure your smartphone or tablet with a strong PIN, password, or biometric authentication. Install security software specifically designed for mobile devices and be cautious of downloading apps from unofficial sources.

Establishing Good Habits and Awareness

Developing good online habits and staying informed about current cybersecurity trends are critical in maintaining your digital security. Regularly educate yourself and your family members about potential threats and safe online practices. Encourage open communication about cybersecurity within your household or workplace to collectively enhance vigilance and preparedness against cyber threats.

Seeking Assistance from Financial Institutions

If you suspect that your financial information has been compromised or notice unusual activity, contact your bank or credit card issuer immediately. Financial institutions have protocols in place to assist customers in resolving fraudulent transactions and securing their accounts. Prompt action can help minimize the impact of cyber incidents on your financial well-being.

Conclusion

In conclusion, while online shopping and banking offer unparalleled convenience, they also require vigilant protection of your personal and financial information. By implementing the strategies outlined in this chapter—such as choosing secure websites, using strong passwords, staying vigilant against phishing, and keeping your devices updated—you can significantly reduce the risks associated with conducting transactions online. Remember, staying informed and proactive is key to enjoying the benefits of digital commerce safely and securely.

Conclusion

In today's interconnected world, safeguarding your computer against viruses, malware, spyware, and adware is not just a matter of convenience but a critical aspect of maintaining digital security. These malicious programs pose significant threats to your personal data, financial information, and overall system integrity.

Throughout this discussion, we have explored various proactive measures to fortify your defenses. Firstly, maintaining robust antivirus and anti-malware software is essential. These tools act as sentinels, constantly scanning for and neutralizing threats before they can infiltrate your system. Regular updates to these programs ensure they are equipped to combat the latest threats effectively.

Moreover, practicing safe browsing habits and exercising caution when downloading files or clicking on links can prevent unwittingly inviting malware into your computer. Avoiding suspicious websites and refraining from downloading software from untrusted sources are simple yet powerful actions to protect against infection.

Understanding the nature of these threats—whether it's the covert data collection of spyware or the intrusive advertisements of adware—empowers users to recognize and mitigate risks effectively. Educating oneself about common attack vectors, such as phishing emails or compromised websites, enhances awareness and resilience against evolving cyber threats.

Furthermore, maintaining a secure network environment, such as using strong passwords and enabling firewalls, creates additional layers of defense against unauthorized access and malware propagation. Regularly backing up important data ensures that even in the event of a successful attack, critical information remains intact and recoverable.

In conclusion, protecting your computer against viruses, malware, spyware, and adware requires a proactive and multi-layered approach. By integrating robust security software, practicing safe browsing habits, staying informed about emerging threats, and maintaining a secure network environment, you significantly reduce the likelihood of falling victim to malicious attacks. Remember, digital security is an ongoing commitment that empowers you to enjoy the benefits of technology safely and confidently.

www.ingramcontent.com/pod-product-compliance
Lightning Source LLC
Chambersburg PA
CBHW060845170526
45158CB00001B/236